THE STRAIGHT AND NARROW ROAD

At each mile
Each year
Old men with closed faces
Point out the road to children
With gestures of reinforced concrete.

—Jacques Prévert
(translation by Lawrence Ferlinghetti)

Barry N. Schwartz

is Assistant Professor of Communication Arts and Skills at New York City Community College and Associate Director of the Center for the Study of Social Change. He has co-edited and authored several volumes, among them *Hard Rains, White Racism, Killing Time, Humanism in 20th-Century Art, Psychedelic Art,* and *America/America,* as well as numerous essays on education and culture.

AFFIRMATIVE EDUCATION

edited by

Barry N. Schwartz

A SPECTRUM BOOK

PRENTICE-HALL, INC. ENGLEWOOD CLIFFS, N.J.

Library of Congress Cataloging in Publication Data

Schwartz, Barry N   comp.
    Affirmative education.

    Includes bibliographical references.
        1. Education—U.S.—1965–   —Addresses, essays,
    lectures. 2. Education—Philosophy—Addresses, essays,
    lectures. I. Title.
    LA217.S3   370.1'0973   72–39863
    ISBN 0–13–018382–2
    ISBN 0–13–018390–3 (pbk.)

"The Straight and Narrow Road" by Jacques Prévert is reprinted from the Pocket Poet Series, *Paroles by Prévert*, by kind permission of City Lights Books, San Francisco. Copyright © 1947 by Les Editions du Point du Jour, Paris.

10 9 8 7 6 5 4 3 2 1

Prentice-Hall International, Inc. (*London*)
Prentice-Hall of Australia Pty. Ltd. (*Sydney*)
Prentice-Hall of Canada Ltd. (*Toronto*)
Prentice-Hall of India Private Limited (*New Delhi*)
Prentice-Hall of Japan, Inc. (*Tokyo*)

Contents

Preface

Young and vociferous antagonists have condemned the activity of education as it is conducted by "the educational establishment." We have witnessed burned buildings, unceasing protest, increasing confrontations, and a few innovative programs. The apologists of the system have chosen to interpret the call for change as nothing less than a mass irrationality that would result in the total destruction of the school and the campus. While the aggrieved and the self-appointed protectors of the schools have shouted themselves into silence the educational system has grueled on indifferently, reacting more to fiscal problems than to all of the turmoil.

The outburst of students and generally younger faculty members can not be explained away as misplaced anger over the war in Vietnam, the ecological crisis, and the existence of institutional racism. This explanation, which sees the school as the unfortunate victim of social evils over which it has no control, does not hold up when contrasted to the deep-seated and pervasive feeling that education is not "relevant," that it is failing a generation that needs it badly. Similarly, the resistance to student demands, to experimentation and a relaxation of the traditional rules can not be accounted for by the fact that teachers are motivated solely by self-interest and an irrational commitment to the status quo. However passionately these positions may be debated it is safe to say that we have seen much rhetoric and little change.

Recently, a long awaited three-and-one-half-year study of American educational institutions terminated with a public announcement of findings. It reported what many critics have long known—that schools are grossly ineffective and that many, perhaps most, do more harm than good. As reported in *The New York Times,* the Carnegie Foundation sponsored report contends "that most schools are preoccupied with order, control and routine for the sake of routine; that students essentially are subjugated by the schools; that by practicing systematic repression, the schools create many of their own discipline problems; and that they promote docility, passivity and conformity in their students." What was novel in the report was not its findings; it was that men who would be the least likely to want to come to these conclusions were as strong in their criticism as those who have been accused of partiality and subjectivity in their analyses of educational institutions. As Charles E. Silberman, senior author of the report, stated, "When we began, I thought the severest critics of the schools were overstating things, but now I think they were understating them."

The credentials of the investigators for this study give assurance of the validity of their findings. The question of whether or not the schools should be dramatically restructured is no longer debatable. The pertinent question is now centered on what changes are needed and how they can be implemented.

It is not the intention of this book to present yet another critique of the educational system. The first brief chapter serves to summarize over a decade of such criticism.

Affirmative education is about changing education. It is the assumption of this book that education needs a new identity first, a new self-image, and that it needs methods by which it can realize this new identity. If education may be thought of as the encounter with lived experience, without the distorting consequences often the result of actual experience, then we may say that affirmative education is a new *way of being* within the educational environment. The many contributions to this book are the bricks with which the foundation of a new educational philosophy can be built. Throughout our nation there are experiments and dedicated experimenters seeking to find an educational behavior that will be the affirmative education we are desperately wanting. This book will bring to study and analysis some of the principles of what emerges as an acceptable liberating education.

The opening section marks the ending of an era in the history of American education—an era that saw unprecedented turmoil and condemnation within an educational system that seemed to serve adequately only two generations ago. The Carnegie Study, authored by Charles E. Silberman, is a synthesis of many of the points raised by the most outspoken critics of the educational establishment; *The New York Times* report on the Commission's findings serves us well as a succinct statement of its major conclusions. In the second section, in a more personal, more experiental, more concrete way, John Holt's essay on "How Children Fail" serves to highlight the severity of the problem while inviting us to begin the search for a more satisfying format for maturation in America.

THIS BOOK IS DEDICATED TO
Robert Disch
who taught me how not to teach
and Katherine Rosenbloom
for her encouragement and assistance on this book

§ THE NEED *for*
AFFIRMATIVE EDUCATION

The educational crisis that has been building since the beginning of the twentieth century has now reached its apex. Ironically, no sooner has the fulfillment of our long-cherished goal of mass education come clearly into sight than the very basis of modern educational theory and practice has begun to be questioned. The principles and assumptions upon which is based the greatest educational system ever constructed are seen, now that that system's achievement seems imminent, to be distorted and invalid for our time.

The reasons for the modern educational predicament are many and varied, but even a cursory analysis reveals that the present crisis is an inevitable outgrowth of historical forces and suggests that it could have been predicted. Education as we know it today came into existence in response to the growing industrialization and technologization of society and to the needs of the new middle class industrial society spawned. Before the Industrial Revolution, the agrarian society had little need for institutionalized education. Formal education before that time had been strictly a pursuit of the aristocracy and the clergy. Most people were "educated" not by schools, but simply by life itself. The family and early work responsibilities taught the average young person all he needed to learn: survival, work, and the social and cultural mores of his time. In medieval society, for example, most of the questions that influence our thought and action today—questions about work, politics, religion, social relationships, and so forth—were answered before birth. For the mass of men education meant learning how to do *well* what it had already been determined they would do. Experience was the best (and probably the only) teacher. Further, since each family's economic goal was self-sufficiency rather than betterment, and since the prices of goods and services were everywhere the same, a child of ten would have learned all he would ever need to know about economics.

All of this leads us to a more general observation: prior to the Renaissance the nature of human life and social experience was more or less constant. The information a person needed for survival and well-being did not change significantly during his lifetime. Since fundamental change was minimal, since the individual functioned within well-defined community and family structures, and since his work was determined by his birth, there was no thought that a person should be taught specific skills and abilities that would enable him to adapt to change. Neither the individual nor the society had a need for mass education.

It is not our purpose here to investigate why this stability ended. Suffice it to say that the growth of cities, the invention of the cannon and the reintroduction of gunpowder, the beginnings of capitalism and surplus economics, and the Protestant Reformation all contributed to the creation of a new world—a world in which change is an everpresent feature. Industrialization threw everything that had been thought to be constant into a state of flux. Simultaneously a new communication medium, print, became a central tool for helping people to understand change. Industrialization required that more and more workers learn increasingly specific skills. As technology continued to change at an ever-increasing rate, it was recognized that human beings would have to be trained to use the new machinery and educated to understand it. The middle class came to regard education as the primary avenue to economic prosperity and social advancement. In an environment fraught with change one had to learn how to adapt, especially since adaptation was thought to be the key to success. In the agrarian system, manual labor and agricultural skills were required; in the new industrial system, technical skills and, after a time, mental labor were required. Yet until very recently it was not recognized that something further was needed to serve the individual in the same way as the family structure and the communal society, which had encouraged healthy personalities and emotional well-being.

Today's crisis can now be simply defined: an educational system built to serve the needs of an industrial society is now asked to serve the needs of a cybernetic society, needs that, oddly enough, are not dissimilar to those of the older agrarian communal society. The present crisis is caused by a serious conflict in educational intentions. Vocational training, literacy, discipline, acculturation to the heritage of post-Renaissance society, and adaptation to cultural and social norms are taught, while "relevancy," environmental perspectives, happiness, personal growth, and personal freedom are demanded.

"Youth in the Technological Era" is my own attempt to describe the strategies that have already been adopted by young people as they come to terms with a world their parents have only known as adults. It is an analysis of values and, if it is correct, it tells us that many of the conventional values upon which the educational system is predicated are presently the victims of wholesale rejection. The essay points to the new kinds of needs associated with a cybernetic time. These needs must be served by a new educational approach if education is to prove relevant and helpful to young people who have to live in the future.

The parent perceives the problem in personal, but equally conflicting, terms. He wants his child to learn what he needs for survival and economic prosperity as they are defined by the existing society. At the same time, he wants his child to be more than a product of his society, with all of its failings and prejudices. The parent has a dim view of contemporary life; he views the world as "tough" and he wants education to teach his child both how to function in it and how to transcend it. In other words, he wants his child to become part of the solution without being victimized by the problem.

It is obvious that the parent's conflicting concerns are a manifestation on the personal level of the crisis that is found throughout society itself: the highest standard of living the world has ever seen coexists with the threat of ecological devastation; the possibility of an end to material deprivation coexists with racial warfare; the global village spends itself on continual war; instantaneous communication coexists with polarization of the population. The parent of today, like parents in any age, wishes the best of his time for his child, yet wants his child to be unscathed by the worst. However, the rate of change today, the magnitude of social problems, and the pervasive confusion in the search for values and meaningful directions greatly intensify the contradictions inherent in what the parent expects from education.

In very general terms, we perceive the conflict as one between the older idea of education as a social control and the newer idea of education as a liberator. In the last decade the desire for liberation and for the development of healthy, integrated personalities has come into direct conflict with the older survival-oriented concept of education as credentials, reality principle, and acculturation process.

As a result, the schools of America are racked with either the pain of breakdown or the disruption of massive resistance, displayed either in excessive absenteeism or in antisocial behavior.

Review of the
Carnegie Commission Report

WILLIAM K. STEVENS

In an unusually outspoken indictment of the nation's public schools, a three-and-a-half-year study commissioned by the Carnegie Corporation has found that most schools not only fail to educate children adequately, but also are "oppressive," "grim" and "joyless" as well.

The study report, written by Charles E. Silberman, an editor, author and former college teacher, is the first of its magnitude and prestige to agree with the severest critics of present American education. Some educators who have read the report expect that it will have major impact on educational debate in the United States.

The report recommends a radical reordering of the classroom along more informal lines, so that a student would be free to use his own interests as a starting point for education and would no longer be dominated by the teacher.

It contends, among other things, that most schools are preoccupied with order, control and routine for the sake of routine; that students essentially are subjugated by the schools; that by practicing systematic repression, the schools create many of their own discipline problems; and that they promote docility, passivity and conformity in their students.

Further, the report charges that students in most classes are taught in a uniform manner, without regard to the individual child's understanding of or interest in a subject; and that despite attempts at reform during the late 1950s and early 1960s, the curriculum in use is often characterized by "banality" and "triviality."

One result of all this, says the report, "is to destroy students' curiosity along with their ability—more serious, their desire—to think and act for themselves." Thereby, it is charged, the schools deny students sufficient ability to understand modern complexity and to translate that understanding into action.

"When we began, I thought the severest critics of the schools were overstating things," Mr. Silberman, director of the study, said in an interview. "But now I think they were understating them."

The gloomy picture is relieved, he writes in the Carnegie report, by examples of successful reform scattered across the country. The schools involved are said to encourage the freedom, informality and individuality associated with the "child-centered" progressive schools of the 1920s and 1930s. But they reportedly avoid the lack of concern with subject matter and intellectual discipline that many believe sent the progressive movement into disrepute.

HOPE AT "INFORMAL SCHOOLS"

Such "informal" schools, the $300,000 Carnegie study concluded, provide models of what education should be, and at the moment offer the main hope for improvement.

The report asserts that reform within the system is possible, in that most teachers and principals would be receptive to the informal approach if they were given the encouragement and support necessary to master it. . . .

"It is clearly one of the best studies on education that has appeared in the last twenty years," said Dr. John Fischer, president of Columbia Teachers College. The study's findings rest on "quite responsible investigation," Dr. Fischer said.

"I think [Mr. Silberman's] findings are quite accurate," said Dr. John I. Goodlad, dean of the Graduate School of Education at the University of California, Los Angeles, one of the country's leading authorities on such issues. "The study gives a clear, comprehensive, sober picture of reality without being a polemic."

In *Crisis in the Classroom*, Mr. Silberman contends that in some respects the schools are better than they ever were before, noting for example, that more people are learning to read. But, in most respects, he charges, the schools are "intolerable."

This is so, he argues, not because teachers are incompetent, indifferent or cruel. Most teachers are characterized by Mr. Silberman as "decent, honest, well-intentioned people" who are victimized by the current system as much as students are.

TEACHERS HELD VICTIMS

The teachers are said to be treated as subservient employees whose job is to take orders and punch the time clock every day, and whose competence is judged not by what and how their students learn, but by how well they control their classes.

The central cause of the difficulty, Mr. Silberman writes, is that schools and teacher training institutions are afflicted by "mindlessness."

By this, he means that educators fail to think seriously about the purposes and consequences of what they do—about the relationship of educational means to ends—and that they seldom question established practice. Lacking any considered philosophy of education, he writes, teachers tend to do what teachers before them have done.

In assailing both the quality of education and the quality of life in the classroom, Mr. Silberman asserts that schools "operate on the assumption of distrust." Teachers assume that pupils cannot be trusted to act in their own best interests, he contends, and principals make similar assumptions about teachers.

This lack of trust produces a kind of school in which virtually every aspect of behavior is governed by minute and petty rules, he argues.

"The most important characteristic the schools share in common is a preoccupation with order and control," the report says. Teachers become primarily disciplinarians, and discipline is defined as "the absence of noise and movement."

Through "the unnatural insistence that children sit silently and motionless," and through "the unreasonable expectation that they will all be interested in the same thing at the same moment and for the same length of time," the report says, the formal classroom seems to produce its own discipline problems—in the form of restlessness, misbehavior and baiting the teacher.

"It is not the children who are disruptive," says the report, "it is the formal classroom that is disruptive—of childhood itself."

Some of this might be tolerated as the price for a "good" academic education, Mr. Silberman writes, except that most students are not getting that, either.

He contends that the high school curriculum reform movement that swept the country around the time of Sputnik I in 1957 "has been blunted on the classroom door"—largely because the reformers, mostly university professors, concentrated on subject matter and paid little attention to how children learn.

"BANALITY AND TRIVIALITY"

In the elementary schools, much of what is taught "is not worth knowing as a child, let alone as an adult, and little will be remembered," Mr. Silberman continues. "The banality and triviality of the curriculum in most schools has to be experienced to be believed."

Furthermore, the report says, schools "discourage students from developing the capacity to learn by and for themselves," because the schools are "structured in such a way as to make students totally dependent upon the teachers." The result is said to be an authoritarian system that "educates for docility."

In examining the schools, Mr. Silberman leaned substantially on the thought of Jean Piaget, the Swiss psychologist who demonstrated, in the words of the Carnegie report, "that the child is the principal agent in his own education and mental development," and that each child's path to understanding is unlike any other child's.

In view of this, Mr. Silberman questions many common assumptions about schooling, including the assumption that "teaching" means teaching a group of students at once from a uniform lesson plan, or any lesson plan at all; and the assumption that all children in a group should be studying the same subject at the same time, even when each child is allowed to go at his own pace in what is often described as "individualized instruction."

"TYRANNY OF LESSON PLAN"

The Carnegie study contends that under the "tyranny of the lesson plan," and of the rigid time schedule it usually requires, lessons often start before children become interested—if, indeed they get interested at all—and end before interest is exhausted or understanding achieved.

In one of more than 200 "items," or concrete examples of school practice that stud the report, Mr. Silberman describes a cluster of children who are "examining a turtle with enormous fascination and intensity." The teacher tells the children to put the turtle away because "we're going to have our science lesson."

In an "informal" or "open" classroom of the kind Mr. Silberman favors as an alternative, the children's natural fascination with the turtle would be used as a springboard into science. But the subject would be pursued only as long as the children were interested. Then each child's ensuing interest would be pursued in a similar manner.

Such schools—operated by ordinary teachers—are said by the Carnegie report to be widely established in England, and to be operating successfully in every section of the United States, although so far they constitute a very small minority in this country.

In such a school, the teacher's job is said to be to apprehend each child's interests and to provide an environment—filled with an abundance of concrete materials and books—to stimulate those interests.

INFORMAL ATMOSPHERE

There is no "up front" in such a classroom, and a teacher seldom teaches a group of children as a whole. There are no rows of desks, and few tables and chairs. The main burden of activity shifts from the teacher to the children, who actively pursue their own interests.

With the burden thus shifted, the teacher finds herself free to work with individual children.

Although such a classroom is child-centered and offers considerable freedom and informality, Mr. Silberman reports, it is not and should not be completely given over to "doing your own thing," as some reformers would favor.

Adults have a responsibility to guide children toward an understanding of the best man has done and thought, the Carnegie report argues. In Mr. Silberman's words, "some things are more important than others and adults have to make conscious choices about which is which" and guide children in the most important directions.

When working with adolescents, who for the first time in their lives are thinking consistently in the abstract, the informal approach might well involve more book work and more conventional research, Mr. Silberman says.

In the high school years, he adds, the teacher has a further responsibility to see that the student acquires the intellectual tools and disciplines that add rigor and validity to inquiry that is fired by natural curiosity.

Mr. Silberman reports that disciplinary and motivational problems largely disappear in informal classrooms; that there is "great joy and spontaneity and activity" coupled with "great self-control and order."

"One simply does not see bored or restless or unhappy youngsters, or youngsters with the glazed look so common in American schools," he writes.

But is informality and joyousness purchased at the price of learning the three R's in the early grades and solid subject-matter in the later years?

Generally, Mr. Silberman reports, "the answer would appear to be no" in the English schools, where the approach has been in effect longest.

Mr. Silberman writes that such schools demonstrate what the American reformer John Dewey argued but many of his disciples ignored— "that a deep and genuine concern for individual growth and fulfillment not only is compatible with but indeed demands an equally genuine concern for cognitive growth and intellectual discipline, for transmitting the cultural heritage of the society."

Youth in the Technological Era

BARRY N. SCHWARTZ

The unique characteristic of the generation now passing through adolescence in America is that it is the first to have been born into a thoroughly technological society, where instantaneous data processing, telstar, atomic energy, moon exploration, push-button warfare, "the pill," and LSD are regarded as environmental facts and not startling innovations. The young are the first generation to experience pervasive technology and affluence as if no other human condition had ever existed. The Depression usually means nothing beyond two pages of a glossy new high school text which will be phased out in two years. Gone is the legendary craftsmanship which produced the enduring appliances their parents so often mourn. Theirs is the world of planned obsolescence and unrelenting change. Because the technological era in which we now live is the only world the young have known, *their values, their sensibilities and their aspirations are distinctly different from those of their parents.* Today many of our youth have only to be alive to be in radical conflict with, and alienated by, the ideas and values of an adult society which prides itself on its luxury and consumes gluttonously.

The parental generation matured in an industrial society striving for the fixed goal of a "higher standard of living," a goal which demanded nose-to-the-grindstone rigidity and strict adherence to prescribed social postures. Our young are growing up in a technological society, soon to become cybernated, which creates ever greater abundance, is conducive to spontaneity, and frees individuals for new ways of thinking and behaving. Consequently, our young live within a different reality from their elders. They sincerely do not feel the sense of the "practical" which characterizes the adult world. Ironically, the drives and personal values of parents who survived a depression and a climb to prosperity are made untenable by their achievement of abundance. The belief that the worth of an individual is determined by his work function and his productivity motivated industrial society toward the present day. But in our affluent age, in which machines will soon produce goods endlessly, such motivations are obsolete.

Nonagrarian economic systems move toward maximizing profit, and today the great obstacle to profit is labor. The cost of raw materials is generally stable; the price of machinery defined and easily absorbed in time; but the cost of labor is an ever-increasing, constantly frustrating, and often unpredictable economic variable. To attain higher profits and greater efficiency, corporations have machines assume the tasks of men. With automation freeing men from their work functions, and with greater quantities of goods available, the value relevant to increasing numbers of young people is not what a man earns by his work, but how satisfying his work is. The current interest in non-specialized education, the creation of interdisciplinary and general "humanities" programs, and the fact that only 12 percent of [1968's] college graduates chose business careers, all reflect a shift in values. Our young constitute the first generation in history to be confronted in the mass by the problem of leisure, and they in turn are challenging society's definition of work.

In the older industrial society objects are the goal of production, a production made possible largely by the expenditure of man's labor. The universal value which necessarily gains ascendancy in such an environment is possession. In the technological era machine-produced objects are abundant and easily replaced, and man is freed from the necessity of laboring to produce in order to consume. As machines assume more of men's productive functions a value based on use rather than possession emerges.

The incentive implicit in the economic system of industrial capitalism is ownership. For the great mass, work is performed in exchange for purchasing power. The young, however, relate to objects as they contribute to individual extension, since most young people are consumers long before they are pressured to become wage earners. These different attitudes and values cause considerable conflict. Many urban adults, for example, take great pleasure in owning a car despite the fact that it may sit idle six days a week. As a possession it is valuable because it symbolizes status and an object achieved. The young are interested in an object as it extends the individual's powers; a car is to go, to be used, and when it is idle it has little importance. Consequently the young use objects in ways adults view as reckless or irresponsible. Because it is important that something be in use, the young often own and use objects communally. In the adult world, where individual possession is a prime value, this kind of multiple extension is not possible.

This difference in values explains why adults collect junk while the young throw things away or "lose" them. Many adults store old or broken objects to be fixed "someday when they may be needed," even though replacement parts may by then be unobtainable. The young discard an unusable object immediately or create a new use for it, perhaps as an art object, in which case it is hung on the wall for display.

This discrepancy between the values of possession and extension also accounts for the change in social relationships. When the adult male was young, he probably valued a woman for her purity. If she was of good reputation, and virgin, the male who won her acquired a possession that was unmarked by previous ownership; she was not "second-hand." If the woman was dull and failed to contribute to the growth of the man, at least she was *his* woman. After marriage he expected fidelity, which affirmed possession. Today among many young men we find that if a woman extends a man, leads him to new experiences, helps him to grow, he is willing to be patient with occasional infidelities or at worst an erratic or difficult relationship. Young women tend to feel similarly.

The sexual mores of the adult world are grounded in a capitalist framework of values which supported the industrial society. Sex is a woman's resource, her labor value, which she invests in amounts sufficient to lead to the desired result—marriage. The idea that she herself could experience pleasure from sex, or even desire this pleasure as an end in itself, threatened the ethical dictates of the adult world. In the past, as theologian Myron Bloy, Jr., suggests, parents used the triple threat of infection, conception, and detection to insure that human relationships arrived at their socially programmed conclusions. But in the technological era the youth have penicillin, contraception, and candor. The life style now emerging among our youth demands that the moment be satisfying, and sex provides a very satisfying moment. The meaning of sex becomes redefined as technology makes it possible as an experience of intrinsic worth.

An industrial society reinforces the very old notion of distinction between the sexes: the man goes to work and is the provider; the woman stays home and cares for the objects and the offspring. The major role relationships between men and women are based on their different work functions. But technological society is breaking down these differing roles. Traditional masculine work is passed on to machines; women's work is greatly reduced by household "labor-saving" machines, nursery schools, and service industries. The qualities usually assigned to men—involvement, logic, imaginative thinking—and to women—sensitivity, perception, warmth, emotion—are now desired in both sexes. The young of both sexes go to school together, work together, and live together. Clothes traditionally assigned exclusively to one sex only are now worn by both, and certain hair styles signify the diminishing of visible difference between them. We can anticipate in the cybernated era that there will be even fewer role distinctions.

Another inherent value of the capitalist system is belief in investment. The adult world encourages the sacrifice of the individual's time and aspiration if it promises future success, where success is usually measured in improved consumer status. In this view man is a means and objects are the end. A man will work thirty-five hours a week for his paycheck. While adult wage earners do what they must, the young, in large part, enjoy the privileges of a leisure class. Millions of them sit in high school and college classrooms getting involved with ideas, activities that after age sixteen would have been inconceivable to any but the sons of the rich only two generations ago. As society achieves greater prosperity, the young enter the work market later and later in life. Consequently, many of the young respond to the values of leisure, not to those of work. Among many, the idea of investing oneself in an uncertain and abstract future has little currency. Indeed, many "dropouts" find it difficult to spend years of their lives in an educational system which values the degree or diploma over the act of learning. Ironically, the result of the older generation's investment makes the principle of investment untenable for its children. The new value, one made wholly practical by a technological era, is that the process itself must satisfy.

Evidence of this emergent value can be seen in the political attitudes of the young. What adult analysts have classified as mere youthful idealism, perhaps in an attempt to dismiss the activist politics of the young altogether, actually represents a philosophical view which sees all men's well-being as the measure. In the politics of the adult world what counts is the result of human activity, a result which may be achieved by lying, by hypocrisy, and by the sacrifice of personal ideals. The investment made is meaningful solely in terms of the success achieved. This concept, root and branch of a capitalist system of economics and morality, defines anything done successfully as inherently good. The politics of youth rejects the idea of investment and demands that the particular act be meaningful. The political process is validated not by the nobility of its ends, but by the authenticity of its means. This is why youthful politics usually are nonideological. Whereas both the Protestant Ethic and Marxism assume that the individual should be subservient to some abstract and overriding end, arguing over which end is just, youth increasingly rejects the adult-projected future along with the past. The present is the only time which can satisfy. This contemporaneity seems reprehensible to those who see history as a continuum.

As I am writing, an important political activity of the young is opposition to the war in Vietnam. Yet rarely does one encounter an individual who believes that he or his group can actually do anything about the war. All the evidence unmistakably indicates that the adult world, the generation in control, is not listening to the protesting young, referred to *en masse* as "prophets of doom." How can one explain the gathering of energies for a cause which its supporters believe cannot succeed? The answer, again, is not youthful idealism, but the fact that the political activity of the young is based less on predictions of success or profit than on a belief that activity itself is affirmative and fulfilling. Protesting a social or political evil, whether the denial of civil rights, war, or illegitimate authority, justifies itself, even if it accomplishes nothing.

This belief in the "rightness" of the act, the demand that the activity itself be fulfilling, leads inevitably to violation of the law. The forms of illegality may be as political as draft-card burning, draft evasion, or disruption of traffic; or as social as underage drinking and the use of drugs; or as private as abortion and sexual deviation. In all cases the law is seen as the coercive arm of the adult world, an aspect of its malignant self-righteousness. Thousands, probably millions, of young people today smoke marijuana in direct violation of laws passed by elders who exist comfortably with abundant alcohol and pep and sedative pills. As many young people feel that before the law is to be respected it must make sense, the unjustified rules that the adult world imposes are flouted with mass irreverence, a social phenomenon for which there can be no effective reprisals. Widespread illegality is but another example that the youth born into a technological society are not compromising with the old industrial society's system. They either confront it openly or subvert it privately, but they seem genuinely unable to accept it.

The dissent of the very young appears in their music. The sounds and lyrics they produce and consume feature improvisation and word combinations nearly unintelligible to adult ears, for the young dislike order and distrust words. Words are the manipulative tools used by Mom and Dad, the System, the Establishment, to herd them into the fold. The new attitudes toward time and activity account for the increasing involvement of youth in the many forms of art. Since the young demand that the moment fulfill, and that the process rather than the result be meaningful, it is inevitable that art is an important part of their life choices. Art, it must be remembered, is that area of human activity in which the values emerging from the youth have been historically significant. Art-as-act is the essence of the artistic experience, one which places the emphasis on creating rather than on what is gained by the activity. Young people will tend to make heroes of artists and emphasize the arts as the technological era makes material existence comfortable and the subjective enjoyment of life viable.

The previous generation, which wished to provide its children with everything they themselves never had, has acclimated the young to plenitude. In the material Eden they have inherited, the young are accustomed to choose what suits them and "turn off" what does not. But it is hard to turn off one's parents. The young and their elders live in the tension created by a vast difference in value systems which has never in history existed between two successive generations in the same society, and the resultant conflict has reached explosive proportions. While the adults seem severe in their judgment and their condemnation, many of the young exhibit a real sense of toleration. While the adult world respects structure, seeing form as all, the young favor content and seek to live in what adults call anarchy. While the adult world finds security in sameness, the young are fascinated with the unusual. While repetitive and familiar experiences usually mark the scope of adult behavior, the young explore the unknown. While most elders want security, most young people are willing to risk. While the elders see virtue in moderation, the young see moderation as inhibiting. While the adults are concerned with the "should," the young are motivated by the "want to." While the older generation assumes an aggressive posture toward different systems and ideas, the young are less willing to leave the conference table for the battlefield.

When young people enter the institutions of the adult world they find that they must conform in order to succeed; their assumption of choice is antithetical to their chances of survival. Some succumb, some rebel. But institutions do not allow dissention. The power which lies in the hands of the older generation coerces obedience with subtle efficiency. The young are often expelled when they demand "relevant" education, outlawed for their private satisfactions, too frequently beaten and jailed for publicly supporting their convictions. . . . The encounter with the adult world is so frequent, so often severe in its consequences and hopeless in its outcome, that youth is plunged into a daily deepening crisis. Given the fact that half the population of the United States is now under twenty-six, this cleavage between the generations would be the most significant internal confrontation in this country were it not for a more overt racial conflict.

For the young, as for all human beings in crisis, there are four possibilities: suicide, escape, rebellion, and submission. It is predicted that five thousand college students will have committed suicide in 1972. But suicide is less desirable in the technological era because another possibility, escape, has become so easy. Geographic escape and mental illness are choices made by many of the young, as the stepped-up exodus to Canada and statistics on adolescent mental disorders indicate. The elaborate psychological services on the campus, the number of "freakouts," the psychological distortions of ghetto youth, all attest to a mode of escape which undeniably signifies damaged personalities. But by far the most popular way of removing oneself from the necessity of responding to an intolerable situation is the drug experience, that inexpensive and not irrevocable transformation of an ugly world into one far more congenial. While drugs do make an oppressive social situation less oppressive, they do not, and cannot, lead to social confrontation, only to social evasion. They are strictly a personal solution. Submission was thoroughly explored by the Silent Generation of the 1950s. The "Now" Generation of the 1960s chose action over passivity, protest over silence. I don't know what the seventies will bring, but we are certainly now witnessing the quiet before the inevitable storm.

The question of how many young people actually constitute the "young" under discussion might fairly be raised. The polarizations and generalities presented here indicate patterns and are not, of course, definitive. These patterns may describe a minority or majority of young people; but that is a moot question. The significant point is that the more vocal and active youth present overtly feelings apparently shared throughout the younger generation. It is certain that the pressures on the young—the draft, institutional authority, manipulation—affect *all* the young. The response to this pressure varies from radical rejection to comfortable acceptance, although Bob Dylan's assertion that "the times, they are a-changing" as manifest in social attitudes, mores, politics, clothing and song, indicates that the latter choice does not essentially represent the way most young people behave. Nor is the adult world properly characterized by a homogeneous attitude, although the behavior of those adults in positions of power and influence betrays apparent similarities of view.

A committed life, and a life which makes little concession to the "practicalities," is possible today without subsequent material hardship. The young can choose for creation, for synthesis of knowledge and experience, and for communication if they are willing to struggle with their parents and the institutions of society; or they can stand passively aside in the belief the old system will destroy itself. Fortunately the technological era is not conducive to passivity. Increasing pressure from above inspires reciprocation from below, and the lines of stress are extending further across existing society.

The young are already the main drive in our society for social change, for equality, and for democracy. It is the young who invigorate the civil rights movement, who demand educational relevance, who serve in the Peace Corps, and who provide the bodies for radical politics. Yet it is problematic whether the young will find the mechanism for directly influencing the direction of our society.

What that influence may mean is the decentralization of massive power, new and meaningful uses of leisure time, education more concerned with understanding and relevance than with sorting and selecting corporate personnel, the revitalization of our cities, a concern for our natural resources, racial integration, human ways of helping the unfortunate, and the search for our society's lost identity and purpose.

The young will either confront society in the hope of changing it, or they will individually and in communities live apart from it. If Marshall McLuhan's predicted humanistic tribalization of society is to occur, it will not happen because the young sit mesmerized before a televised stream of trivia, but because dedicated and intelligent young men and women, using the tools of the technological era, will attempt to refashion society. For this to happen the new values now exhibited negatively as dissent must be transformed into positive realizations. One dissents *from,* but rebels *for.* Whatever their decision, it will indelibly alter the fate of our world.

§ THE BASIS for AFFIRMATIVE EDUCATION

The earliest known writings on education come from fifth-century Greece. The Greeks carried on a healthy debate about education, but certain general characteristics of their educational philosophy can be isolated. What stands out most prominently is the assumption that education, an integrated, holistic personality, and good citizenship were fundamentally related. Education was supposed to accentuate those human qualities that, once developed, would yield the good life, personal happiness, and a vital society. The goal was neither intelligence nor mental proficiency, but wisdom, or, short of that, well-being while in the pursuit of wisdom.

The Christian era, in the first dramatic departure from the Classical model, focused education not on the individual but on the "truths" of the Christian world view. Although one may consider the Christian contribution to educational theory to be an affirmation of the soul as a vital part of the human presence, these "truths" were not to be discovered through spontaneous individual processes but merely by "learning" what was already "known."

In the Renaissance we see the emergence of humanistic education —the joy of discovering antiquity and classical literature. Unfortunately this joy was limited to those who were capable of translating Greek and Latin or who possessed the money to buy such translations in handwritten manuscripts. In either case, such studies required available leisure time and thus excluded the mass of men.

One of the chief features of the post-Renaissance period is the insistence by the middle class that many things that were once prerogatives of the aristocracy be made available to all. Thus almost from the start mass education stressed the "great books" or humanities approach to education that resembled the Renaissance discovery of antiquity. The specific dangers of this kind of curriculum can be deduced from John Holt's comments about curriculum in general.

Clearly the greatest inheritance from the Renaissance is not the curriculum inherited from the studies of the aristocracy, but the movable type printing press. Gutenberg's invention created a new medium and the Protestant Reformation gave it its earliest application. Literacy was first encouraged so that people would be able to read the Bible, a necessity according to the precepts of Protestantism. Eventually, however, the medium itself proved to be more potent than the particular content it served to convey. In a relatively short time literacy became the point around which numerous educational theories and practices rotated. Focusing on literacy insured that education would come to be considered the primary way to achieve wealth and social mobility.

As in the Christian era, the educational emphasis in the nineteenth century turned away from personal growth and discovery toward more utilitarian purposes. Industrialism required literacy, technical capabilities, and a concept of citizenship defined by laissez-faire economics and libertarian ideals. Education and schooling began to become synonymous and, though not everyone was able to go to school, the ideal of school became widely accepted. Whereas the aim of Renaissance learning had been more rewarding living, the aim of nineteenth-century learning, except for the very wealthy, became more vocational. Vocational influences in educational theory led to the universal application of the memorization methodology we see still prevalent.

No single factor exercised so strong an influence on the developing twentieth-century concept of education as the burgeoning art or science of psychology. Here was a field that paid respect to the inner workings of the mind, to the ill-defined boundaries between emotion and intellect, and to the stirrings of internal forces that were found to have greater impact upon human behavior than had ever been thought. The psychological perspective sees the teacher not as one who merely imparts knowledge and assesses the degree to which the students have incorporated what was taught, but more as someone who is adept at promoting personal growth among children. Thus a psychological approach urges a teacher to learn about his or her students, while a utilitarian approach wants a teacher to provide what it is believed the students need to know about the world. The influence of psychology on educational theory led to a sensitivity to process and to developmental patterns, in contrast to a concentration on a fixed body of knowledge that must be transmitted if the student is to overcome his abysmal ignorance and assume his "rightful" place in the world.

Today's educational ferment is in one sense a battle between the utilitarian tradition of the nineteenth century and the spreading new educational theories that incorporate the insights of psychological knowledge. This conflict has intensified greatly since the launching of Sputnik I, which sent tremors of utilitarian influence shooting through educational practice.

Affirmative education, as described in this book, attempts to syr thesize the psychoanalytic insights of the twentieth century and the more worldly aspirations of the fifth-century Greeks in the hope that the combination will enable young people to live in the future. It sees *both* personal growth, stimulated by inner mechanisms, and the relation between the individual and society, stimulated by concrete and meaningful interactions, as primary bases for an educational theory and a methodology. It is in this sense that Holt defines intelligence as "a style of life, a way of behaving in various situations, and particularly in new, strange, and perplexing situations. The true test of intelligence is not how much we know how to do, but how we behave when we don't know what to do." This view of education is relevant to both the present and the future. It is based on the assumption, discussed by Postman and Weingartner, that *"what you have is a totally new environment requiring a whole new repertoire of survival strategies."* In fact, Holt's essay may be read as a list of do's and don'ts. The do's are what affirmative education is about and the don'ts are descriptions of present-day educational practices. We will concentrate on the do's. Holt argues that there must be no wall, no barrier to prevent interaction between individuals and life. And as we shall see later, affirmative education requires that the subject of education, its "content," be that very interaction.

This view holds that facts become useful only as they promote a positive interaction. It also refuses to pay homage to the god of competition and considers "the feeling that they are better than someone else" to be utterly destructive. Affirmative education does not lend itself to fragmentation, "breaking up life into arbitrary and disconnected chunks of subject matter." John Holt's do's are given the rationale they require in the essays that follow.

Neil Postman and Charles Weingartner have been instrumental in translating sociological insights into educational philosophy. Their essay on "Crap Detecting" is unflinching in its position that our new era, characterized by *an increasing rate of change,* has made current educational philosophy obsolete. They create a solid foundation for affirmative education, reminding us that the children in today's classrooms are destined to live in a world their teachers will never really know.

The focal point of Part Two is George Leonard's "What Is Education," which fully articulates the general requirements of affirmative education. Leonard incorporates the positions of Postman and Weingartner and presents some of the basic tenets that must become standard operating insights when we teach and "educate" if we are to be of genuine value to young people.

It follows from Leonard's essay that teachers must know equally well what to put in and what to draw out. The teacher must respect a meaningful balance between intellect and feeling, judgment and curiosity. He must know that education is based on the understanding of children and the ways they learn. If he thinks of his students as immature adults who must, through his effort, become mature adults or learn about the rich heritage that has been bequeathed to them or gain the skills necessary for the jobs their fathers want them to have, he will fail to ignite that special experience we are striving for. If, on the other hand, the teacher sees the classroom as a place to encourage personal growth, creativity, and the will to explore fully, he will be receptive to the various arguments offered here.

As a last contribution to Part Two I include R. D. Laing's discussion of experience. Since affirmative education wishes to develop? encourage? emphasize? experience and remove the barriers between life and learning, we must become fully aware of how barriers are constructed. Laing's essay, though difficult, is a relentless investigation of how experience is destroyed. The teacher who wishes to participate in affirmative education as it is suggested here must be well informed about how we handle experience itself.

How Children Fail

JOHN HOLT

When we talk about intelligence, we do not mean the ability to get
a good score on a certain kind of test, or even the ability to do well
in school; these are at best only indicators of something larger, deeper,
and far more important. By intelligence we mean a style of life, a way
of behaving in various situations, and particularly in new, strange, and
perplexing situations. The true test of intelligence is not how much
we know how to do, but how we behave when we don't know what
to do.

The intelligent person, young or old, meeting a new situation or
problem, opens himself up to it; he tries to take in with mind and
senses everything he can about it; he thinks about *it,* instead of about
himself or what it might cause to happen to him; he grapples with it
boldly, imaginatively, resourcefully, and if not confidently at least
hopefully; if he fails to master it, he looks without shame or fear at
his mistakes and learns what he can from them. This is intelligence.
Clearly its roots lie in a certain feeling about life, and one's self with
respect to life. Just as clearly, unintelligence is not what most psychologists seem to suppose, the same thing as intelligence only less of it.
It is an entirely different style of behavior, arising out of an entirely
different set of attitudes.

Years of watching and comparing bright children and the not-bright,
or less bright, have shown that they are very different kinds of people.
The bright child is curious about life and reality, eager to get in touch
with it, embrace it, unite himself with it. There is no wall, no barrier
between him and life. The dull child is far less curious, far less interested in what goes on and what is real, more inclined to live in worlds
of fantasy. The bright child likes to experiment, to try things out. He
lives by the maxim that there is more than one way to skin a cat. If
he can't do something one way, he'll try another. The dull child is

usually afraid to try at all. It takes a good deal of urging to get him to try even once; if that try fails, he is through.

The bright child is patient. He can tolerate uncertainty and failure, and will keep trying until he gets an answer. When all his experiments fail, he can even admit to himself and others that for the time being he is not going to get an answer. This may annoy him, but he can wait. Very often, he does not want to be told how to do the problem or solve the puzzle he has struggled with, because he does not want to be cheated out of the chance to figure it out for himself in the future. Not so the dull child. He cannot stand uncertainty or failure. To him, an unanswered question is not a challenge or an opportunity, but a threat. If he can't find the answer quickly, it must be given to him, and quickly; and he must have answers for everything. Such are the children of whom a second-grade teacher once said, "But my children *like* to have questions for which there is only one answer." They did; and by a mysterious coincidence, so did she.

The bright child is willing to go ahead on the basis of incomplete understanding and information. He will take risks, sail uncharted seas, explore when the landscape is dim, the landmarks few, the light poor. To give only one example, he will often read books he does not understand in the hope that after a while enough understanding will emerge to make it worth while to go on. In this spirit some of my fifth graders tried to read *Moby Dick*. But the dull child will go ahead only when he thinks he knows exactly where he stands and exactly what is ahead of him. If he does not feel he knows exactly what an experience will be like, and if it will not be exactly like other experiences he already knows, he wants no part of it. For while the bright child feels that the universe is, on the whole, a sensible, reasonable, and trustworthy place, the dull child feels that it is senseless, unpredictable, and treacherous. He feels that he can never tell what may happen, particularly in a new situation, except that it will probably be bad.

Nobody starts off stupid. You have only to watch babies and infants, and think seriously about what all of them learn and do, to see that, except for the most grossly retarded, they show a style of life, and a desire and ability to learn that in an older person we might well call genius. Hardly an adult in a thousand, or ten thousand, could in any three years of his life learn as much, grow as much in his understanding of the world around him, as every infant learns and grows in his first three years. But what happens, as we get older, to this extraordinary capacity for learning and intellectual growth?

What happens is that it is destroyed, and more than by any other one thing, by the process that we misname education—a process that goes on in most homes and schools. We adults destroy most of the intellectual and creative capacity of children by the things we do to them or make them do. We destroy this capacity above all by making them afraid, afraid of not doing what other people want, of not pleasing, of making mistakes, of failing, of being *wrong*. Thus we make them afraid to gamble, afraid to experiment, afraid to try the difficult and the unknown. Even when we do not create children's fears, when they come to us with fears ready-made and built-in, we use these fears as handles to manipulate them and get them to do what we want. Instead of trying to whittle down their fears, we build them up, often to monstrous size. For we like children who are a little afraid of us, docile, deferential children, though not, of course, if they are so obviously afraid that they threaten our image of ourselves as kind, lovable people whom there is no reason to fear. We find ideal the kind of "good" children who are just enough afraid of us to do everything we want, without making us feel that fear of us is what is making them do it.

We destroy the disinterested (I do *not* mean *un*interested) love of learning in children, which is so strong when they are small, by encouraging and compelling them to work for petty and contemptible rewards—gold stars, or papers marked 100 and tacked to the wall, or *A*'s on report cards, or honor rolls, or dean's lists, or Phi Beta Kappa keys—in short, for the ignoble satisfaction of feeling that they are better than someone else. We encourage them to feel that the end and aim of all they do in school is nothing more than to get a good mark on a test, or to impress someone with what they seem to know. We kill, not only their curiosity, but their feeling that it is a good and admirable thing to be curious, so that by the age of ten most of them will not ask questions, and will show a good deal of scorn for the few who do.

In many ways, we break down children's convictions that things make sense, or their hope that things may prove to make sense. We do it, first of all, by breaking up life into arbitrary and disconnected hunks of subject matter, which we then try to "integrate" by such artificial and irrelevant devices as having children sing Swiss folk songs while they are studying the geography of Switzerland, or do arithmetic problems about rail-splitting while they are studying the boyhood of Lincoln. Furthermore, we continually confront them with what is senseless, ambiguous, and contradictory; worse, we do it without knowing that we are doing it, so that, hearing nonsense shoved at them as if it were sense, they come to feel that the source of their confusion lies not in the material but in their own stupidity. Still further, we cut children off from their own common sense and the world of reality by requiring them to play with and shove around words and symbols that have little or no meaning to them. Thus we turn the vast majority of our students into the kind of people for whom all symbols are meaningless; who cannot use symbols as a way of learning about and dealing with reality; who cannot understand written instructions; who, even if they read books, come out knowing no more than when they went in; who may have a few new words rattling around in their heads, but whose mental models of the world remain unchanged and, indeed, impervious to change. The minority, the able and successful students, we are very likely to turn into something different but just as dangerous: the kind of people who can manipulate words and symbols fluently while keeping themselves largely divorced from the reality for which they stand; the kind of people who like to speak in large generalities but grow silent or indignant if someone asks for an example of what they are talking about; the kind of people who, in their discussions of world affairs, coin and use such words as megadeaths and megacorpses, with scarcely a thought to the blood and suffering these words imply.

We encourage children to act stupidly, not only by scaring and confusing them, but by boring them, by filling up their days with dull, repetitive tasks that make little or no claim on their attention or demands on their intelligence. Our hearts leap for joy at the sight of a roomful of children all slogging away at some imposed task, and we are all the more pleased and satisfied if someone tells us that the children don't really like what they are doing. We tell ourselves that this drudgery, this endless busywork, is good preparation for life, and we fear that without it children would be hard to "control." But why must this busywork be so dull? Why not give tasks that are interesting and demanding? Because, in schools where every task must be completed and every answer must be right, if we give children more demanding tasks they will be fearful and will instantly insist that we show them how to do the job. When you have acres of paper to fill up with pencil marks, you have no time to waste on the luxury of thinking. By such means children are firmly established in the habit of using only a small part of their thinking capacity. They feel that school is a place where they must spend most of their time doing dull tasks in a dull way. Before long they are deeply settled in a rut of unintelligent behavior from which most of them could not escape even if they wanted to.

School tends to be a dishonest as well as a nervous place. We adults are not often honest with children, least of all in school. We tell them, not what we think, but what we feel they ought to think; or what other people feel or tell us they ought to think. Pressure groups find it easy to weed out of our classrooms, texts, and libraries whatever facts, truths, and ideas they happen to find unpleasant or inconvenient. And we are not even as truthful with children as we could safely be, as the parents, politicians, and pressure groups would let us be. Even in the most noncontroversial areas our teaching, the books, and the textbooks we give children present a dishonest and distorted picture of the world.

The fact is that we do not feel an obligation to be truthful to children. We are like the managers and manipulators of news in Washington, Moscow, London, Peking, and Paris, and all the other capitals of the world. We think it our right and our duty, not to tell the truth, but to say whatever will best serve our cause—in this case, the cause of making children grow up into the kind of people we want them to be, thinking whatever we want them to think. We have only to convince ourselves (and we are very easily convinced) that a lie will be "better" for the children than the truth, and we will lie. We don't always need even that excuse; we often lie only for our own convenience. . . .

We are, above all, dishonest about our feelings, and it is this sense of dishonesty of feeling that makes the atmosphere of so many schools so unpleasant. The people who write books that teachers have to read say over and over again that a teacher must love all the children in a class, all of them equally. If by this they mean that a teacher must do the best he can for every child in a class, that he has an equal responsibility for every child's welfare, an equal concern for his problems, they are right. But when they talk of love they don't mean this; they mean feelings, affection, the kind of pleasure and joy that one person can get from the existence and company of another. And this is not something that can be measured out in little spoonfuls, everyone getting the same amount. . . .

Behind much of what we do in school lie some ideas, that could be expressed roughly as follows: (1) Of the vast body of human knowledge, there are certain bits and pieces that can be called essential, that everyone should know; (2) the extent to which a person can be considered educated, qualified to live intelligently in today's world and be a useful member of society, depends on the amount of this essential knowledge that he carries about with him; (3) it is the duty of schools, therefore, to get as much of this essential knowledge as possible into the minds of children. Thus we find ourselves trying to poke certain facts, recipes, and ideas down the gullets of every child in school, whether the morsel interests him or not, even if it frightens him or sickens him, and even if there are other things that he is much more interested in learning.

These ideas are absurd and harmful nonsense. We will not begin to have true education or real learning in our schools until we sweep this nonsense out of the way. Schools should be a place where children learn what they most want to know, instead of what we think they ought to know. The child who wants to know something remembers it and uses it once he has it; the child who learns something to please or appease someone else forgets it when the need for pleasing or the danger of not appeasing is past. This is why children quickly forget all but a small part of what they learn in school. It is of no use or interest to them; they do not want, or expect, or even intend to remember it. The only difference between bad and good students in this respect is that the bad students forget right away, while the good students are careful to wait until after the exam. If for no other reason, we could well afford to throw out most of what we teach in school because the children throw out almost all of it anyway.

The notion of a curriculum, an essential body of knowledge, would be absurd even if children remembered everything we "taught" them. We don't and can't agree on what knowledge is essential. The man who has trained himself in some special field of knowledge or competence thinks, naturally, that his specialty should be in the curriculum. The classical scholars want Greek and Latin taught; the historians shout for more history; the mathematicians urge more math and the scientists more science; the modern language experts want all children taught French, or Spanish, or Russian; and so on. Everyone wants to get his specialty into the act, knowing that as the demand for his special knowledge rises, so will the price that he can charge for it. Who wins this struggle and who loses depends not on the real needs of children or even of society, but on who is most skillful in public relations, who has the best educational lobbyists, who best can capitalize on events that have nothing to do with education, like the appearance of Sputnik in the night skies.

The idea of the curriculum would not be valid even if we could agree what ought to be in it. For knowledge itself changes. Much of what a child learns in school will be found, or thought, before many years, to be untrue. I studied physics at school from a fairly up-to-date text that proclaimed that the fundamental law of physics was the law of conservation of matter—matter is not created or destroyed. I had to scratch that out before I left school. In economics at college I was taught many things that were not true of our economy then, and many more that are not true now. Not for many years after I left college did I learn that the Greeks, far from being a detached and judicious people surrounded by chaste white temples, were hot-tempered, noisy, quarrelsome, and liked to cover their temples with gold leaf and bright paint; or that most of the citizens of Imperial Rome, far from living in houses in which the rooms surrounded an atrium, or central court, lived in multistory tenements, one of which was perhaps the largest building in the ancient world. The child who really remembered everything he heard in school would live his life believing many things that were not so. . . .

How can we say, in any case, that one piece of knowledge is more important than another, or indeed, what we really say, that some knowledge is essential and the rest, as far as school is concerned, worthless? A child who wants to learn something that the school can't and doesn't want to teach him will be told not to waste his time. But how can we say that what he wants to know is less important than what we want him to know? We must ask how much of the sum of human knowledge anyone can know at the end of his schooling. Perhaps a millionth. Are we then to believe that one of these millionths is so much more important than another? Or that our social and national problems will be solved if we can just figure out a way to turn children out of schools knowing two millionths of the total, instead of one? Our problems don't arise from the fact that we lack experts enough to tell us what needs to be done, but out of the fact that we do not and will not do what we know needs to be done now. . . .

It is not subject matter that makes some learning more valuable than others, but the spirit in which the work is done. If a child is doing the kind of learning that most children do in school, when they learn at all—swallowing words, to spit back at the teacher on demand —he is wasting his time, or rather, we are wasting it for him. This learning will not be permanent, or relevant, or useful. But a child who is learning naturally, following his curiosity where it leads him, adding to his mental model of reality whatever he needs and can find a place for, and rejecting without fear or guilt what he does not need, is growing—in knowledge, in the love of learning, and in the ability to learn. He is on his way to becoming the kind of person we need in our society, and that our "best" schools and colleges are *not* turning out, the kind of person who, in Whitney Griswold's words, seeks and finds meaning, truth, and enjoyment in everything he does. All his life he will go on learning. Every experience will make his mental model of reality more complete and more true to life, and thus make him more able to deal realistically, imaginatively, and constructively with whatever new experience life throws his way.

We cannot have real learning in school if we think it is our duty and our right to tell children what they must learn. We cannot know, at any moment, what particular bit of knowledge or understanding a child needs most, will most strengthen and best fit his model of reality. Only he can do this. He may not do it very well, but he can do it a hundred times better than we can. The most we can do is try to help, by letting him know roughly what is available and where he can look for it. Choosing what he wants to learn and what he does not is something he must do for himself.

There is one more reason, and the most important one, why we must reject the idea of school and classroom as places where, most of the time, children are doing what some adult tells them to do. The reason is that there is no way to coerce children without making them afraid, or more afraid. We must not try to fool ourselves into thinking that this is not so. The would-be progressives, who until recently had great influence over most American public school education, did not recognize this—and still do not. They thought, or at least talked and wrote as if they thought, that there were good ways and bad ways to coerce children (the bad ones mean, harsh, cruel, the good ones gentle, persuasive, subtle, kindly), and that if they avoided the bad and stuck to the good they would do no harm. This was one of their greatest mistakes, and the main reason why the revolution they hoped to accomplish never took hold.

The idea of painless, nonthreatening coercion is an illusion. Fear is the inseparable companion of coercion, and its inescapable consequence. If you think it your duty to make children do what you want, whether they will or not, then it follows inexorably that you must make them afraid of what will happen to them if they don't do what you want. You can do this in the old-fashioned way, openly and avowedly, with the threat of harsh words, infringement of liberty, or physical punishment. Or you can do it in the modern way, subtly, smoothly, quietly, by withholding the acceptance and approval which you and others have trained the children to depend on; or by making them feel that some retribution awaits them in the future, too vague to imagine but too implacable to escape. You can, as many skilled teachers do, learn to tap with a word, a gesture, a look, even a smile, the great reservoir of fear, shame, and guilt that today's children carry around inside them. Or you can simply let your own fears, about what will happen to you if the children don't do what you want, reach out and infect them. Thus the children will feel more and more that life is full of dangers from which only the good will of adults like you can protect them, and that this good will is perishable and must be earned anew each day.

The alternative—I can see no other—is to have schools and classrooms in which each child in his own way can satisfy his curiosity, develop his abilities and talents, pursue his interests, and from the adults and older children around him get a glimpse of the great variety and richness of life. In short, the school should be a great smörgåsbord of intellectual, artistic, creative, and athletic activities, from which each child could take whatever he wanted, and as much as he wanted, or as little. When Anna was in the sixth grade, the year after she was in my class, I mentioned this idea to her. After describing very sketchily how such a school might be run, and what the children might do, I said, "Tell me, what do you think of it? Do you think it would work? Do you think the kids would learn anything?" She said, with utmost conviction, "Oh, yes, it would be wonderful!" She was silent for a minute or two, perhaps remembering her own generally unhappy schooling. Then she said thoughtfully, "You know, kids really like to learn; we just don't like being pushed around."

No, they don't; and we should be grateful for that. So let's stop pushing them around, and give them a chance.

Crap Detecting

NEIL POSTMAN AND
CHARLES WEINGARTNER

"In 1492, Columbus discovered America. . . ." Starting from this disputed fact, each one of us will describe the history of this country in a somewhat different way. Nonetheless, it is reasonable to assume that most of us would include something about what is called the "democratic process," and how Americans have valued it, or at least have said they valued it. Therein lies a problem: one of the tenets of a democratic society is that men be allowed to think and express themselves freely on any subject, even to the point of speaking out against the idea of a democratic society. To the extent that our schools are instruments of such a society, they must develop in the young not only an awareness of this freedom but a will to exercise it, and the intellectual power and perspective to do so effectively. This is necessary so that the society may continue to change and modify itself to meet unforeseen threats, problems, and opportunities. Thus, we can achieve what John Gardner calls an "ever-renewing society."

So goes the theory.

In practice, we mostly get a different story. In our society, as in others, we find that there are influential men at the head of important institutions who cannot afford to be found wrong, who find change inconvenient, perhaps intolerable, and who have financial or political interests they must conserve at any cost. Such men are, therefore, threatened in many respects by the theory of the democratic process and the concept of an ever-renewing society. Moreover, we find that there are obscure men who do *not* head important institutions who are similarly threatened because they have identified themselves with certain ideas and institutions which they wish to keep free from either criticism or change.

Such men as these would much prefer that the schools do little or nothing to encourage youth to question, doubt, or challenge any part

"Crap Detecting." From Neil Postman and Charles Weingartner, *Teaching as a Subversive Activity* (New York: Delacorte Press, 1969), pp. 1–15. Copyright © 1969 by Neil Postman and Charles Weingartner. Reprinted by permission of the publisher.

of the society in which they live, especially those parts which are most vulnerable. "After all," say the practical men, "they are *our* schools, and they ought to promote *our* interests, and *that* is part of the democratic process, too." True enough; and here we have a serious point of conflict. Whose schools are they, anyway, and whose interests should they be designed to serve? We realize that these are questions about which any self-respecting professor of education could write several books, each one beginning with a reminder that the problem is not black or white, either/or, yes or no. But . . . you [should] not expect us to be either professorial or prudent. We are, after all, trying to suggest strategies for survival as they may be developed in our schools, and the situation requires emphatic responses. We believe that the schools must serve as the principal medium for developing in youth the attitudes and skills of social, political, and cultural criticism. No. That is not emphatic enough. Try this: In the early 1960s, an interviewer was trying to get Ernest Hemingway to identify the characteristics required for a person to be a "great writer." As the interviewer offered a list of various possibilities, Hemingway disparaged each in sequence. Finally, frustrated, the interviewer asked, "Isn't there any one essential ingredient that you can identify?" Hemingway replied, "Yes, there is. In order to be a great writer a person must have a built-in, shockproof crap detector."

It seems to us that, in his response, Hemingway identified an essential survival strategy and the essential function of the schools in today's world. One way of looking at the history of the human group is that it has been a continuing struggle against the veneration of "crap." Our intellectual history is a chronicle of the anguish and suffering of men who tried to help their contemporaries see that some part of their fondest beliefs were misconceptions, faulty assumptions, superstitions, and even outright lies. The mileposts along the road of our intellectual development signal those points at which some person developed a new perspective, a new meaning, or a new metaphor. We have in mind a new education that would set out to cultivate just such people —experts at "crap detecting."

There are many ways of describing this function of the schools, and many men who have. David Riesman, for example, calls this the "countercyclical" approach to education, meaning that schools should stress values that are not stressed by other major institutions in the culture. Norbert Wiener insisted that the schools now must function as "antientropic feedback systems," "entropy" being the word used to denote a general and unmistakable tendency of all systems—natural and man-made—in the universe to "run down," to reduce to chaos and uselessness. This is a process that cannot be reversed but that can be slowed down and partly controlled. One way to control it is through "maintenance." This is Eric Hoffer's term, and he believes that the quality of maintenance is one of the best indices of the quality of life in a culture. But Wiener uses a different metaphor to get at the same idea. He says that in order for there to be an antientropic force, we must have adequate feedback. In other words, we must have instruments to tell us when we are running down, when maintenance is required. For Wiener, such instruments would be people who have been educated to recognize change, to be sensitive to problems caused by change, and who have the motivation and courage to sound alarms when entropy accelerates to a dangerous degree. This is what we mean by "crap detecting." It is also what John Gardner means by the "ever-renewing society," and what Kenneth Boulding means by "social self-consciousness." We are talking about the schools' cultivating in the young that most "subversive" intellectual instrument—the anthropological perspective. This perspective allows one to be part of his own culture and, at the same time, to be out of it. One views the activities of his own group as would an anthropologist, observing its tribal rituals, its fears, its conceits, its ethnocentrism. In this way, one is able to recognize when reality begins to drift too far away from the grasp of the tribe.

We need hardly say that achieving such a perspective is extremely difficult, requiring, among other things, considerable courage. We are, after all, talking about achieving a high degree of freedom from the intellectual and social constraints of one's tribe. For example, it is generally assumed that people of other tribes have been victimized by indoctrination from which our tribe has remained free. Our own outlook seems "natural" to us, and we wonder that other men can perversely persist in believing nonsense. Yet, it is undoubtedly true that, for most people, the acceptance of a particular doctrine is largely attributable to the accident of birth. They might be said to be "ideologically interchangeable," which means that they would have accepted any set of doctrines that happened to be valued by the tribe to which they were born. Each of us, whether from the American tribe, Russian tribe, or Hopi tribe, is born into a symbolic environment as well as a physical one. We become accustomed very early to a "natural" way of talking, and being talked to, about "truth." Quite arbitrarily, one's perception of what is "true" or real is shaped by the symbols and symbol-manipulating institutions of his tribe. Most men, in time, learn to respond with fervor and obedience to a set of verbal abstractions which they feel provides them with an ideological identity. One word for this, of course, is "prejudice." None of us is free of it, but it is the sign of a competent "crap detector" that he is not completely captivated by the arbitrary abstractions of the community in which he happened to grow up.

In our own society, if one grows up in a language environment which includes and approves such a concept as "white supremacy," one can quite "morally" engage in the process of murdering civil-rights workers. Similarly, if one is living in a language environment where the term "black power" crystallizes an ideological identity, one can engage, again quite "morally," in acts of violence against any nonblack persons or their property. An insensitivity to the unconscious effects of our "natural" metaphors condemns us to highly constricted perceptions of how things are and, therefore, to highly limited alternative modes of behavior.

Those who *are* sensitive to the verbally built-in biases of their "natural" environment seem "subversive" to those who are not. There is probably nothing more dangerous to the prejudices of the latter than a man in the process of discovering that the language of his group is limited, misleading, or one-sided. Such a man is dangerous because he is not easily enlisted on the side of one ideology or another, because he sees beyond the words to the processes which give an ideology its reality. In his *May Man Prevail?*, Erich Fromm gives us an example of a man (himself) in the process of doing just that:

> The Russians believe that they represent socialism because they talk in terms of Marxist ideology, and they do not recognize how similar their system is to the most developed form of capitalism. We in the West believe that we represent the system of individualism, private initiative, and humanistic ethics, because we hold on to *our* ideology, and we do not see that our institutions have, in fact, in many ways become more and more similar to the hated system of communism.

Religious indoctrination is still another example of this point. As Alan Watts has noted: "Irrevocable commitment to any religion is not only intellectual suicide; it is positive unfaith because it closes the mind to any new vision of the world. Faith is, above all, openness—an act of trust in the unknown." And so "crap detecting" requires a perspective on what Watts calls "the standard-brand religions." That perspective can also be applied to knowledge. If you substitute the phrase "set of facts" for the word "religion" in the quotation above, the statement is equally important and accurate.

The need for this kind of perspective has always been urgent but never so urgent as now. . . . Three particular problems . . . force us to conclude that the schools must consciously remake themselves into training centers for "subversion." In one sense, they are all one problem but for purposes of focus may be distinguished from each other.

The first goes under the name of the "communications revolution," or media change. As Father John Culkin of Fordham University likes to say, a lot of things have happened in this century and most of them plug into walls. To get some perspective on the electronic plug, imagine that your home and all the other homes and buildings in your neighborhood have been cordoned off, and from them will be removed all the electric and electronic inventions that have appeared in the last fifty years. The media will be subtracted in reverse order, with the most recent going first. The first thing to leave your house, then, is the television set—and everybody will stand there as if they are attending the funeral of a friend, wondering, "What are we going to do tonight?" After rearranging the furniture so that it is no longer aimed at a blank space in the room, you suggest going to the movies. But there won't be any. Nor will there be LP records, tapes, radio, telephone, or telegraph. If you are thinking that the absence of the media would only affect your entertainment and information, remember that, at some point, your electric lights would be removed, and your refrigerator, and your heating system, and your air conditioner. In short, you would have to be a totally different person from what you are in order to survive for more than a day. The chances are slim that you could modify yourself and your patterns of living and believing fast enough to save yourself. As you were expiring, you would at least know something about how it was before the electric plug. Or perhaps you wouldn't. In any case, if you had energy and interest enough to hear him, any good ecologist could inform you of the logic of your problem: a change in an environment is rarely only additive or linear. You seldom, if ever, have an old environment *plus* a new element, such as a printing press or an electric plug. *What you have is a totally new environment requiring a whole new repertoire of survival strategies.* In no case is this more certain than when the new elements are technological. Then, in no case will the new environment be more radically different from the old than in political and social forms of life. When you plug something into a wall, someone is getting plugged into you. Which means you need new patterns of defense, perception, understanding, evaluation. You need a new kind of education.

It was George Counts who observed that technology repealed the Bill of Rights. In the eighteenth century, a pamphlet could influence an entire nation. Today all the ideas of the Noam Chomskys, Paul Goodmans, Edgar Friedenbergs, I. F. Stones, and even the William Buckleys, cannot command as much attention as a 30-minute broadcast by Walter Cronkite. Unless, of course, one of them were given a prime-time network program, in which case he would most likely come out more like Walter Cronkite than himself. Even Marshall McLuhan, who is leading the field in understanding media, is having his ideas transformed and truncated by the forms of the media to fit present media functions. (One requirement, for example, is that an idea or a man must be "sensational" in order to get a hearing; thus, McLuhan comes out not as a scholar studying media but as the "Apostle of the Electronic Age.")

We trust it is clear that we are not making the typical, whimpering academic attack on the media. We are not "against" the media. Any more, incidentally, than McLuhan is "for" the media. You cannot reverse technological change. Things that plug in are here to stay. But you can study media, with a view toward discovering what they are doing to you. As McLuhan has said, there is no inevitability so long as there is a willingness to contemplate what is happening.

Very few of us have contemplated more rigorously what is happening through media change than Jacques Ellul, who has sounded some chilling alarms. Without mass media, Ellul insists, there can be no effective propaganda. With them, there is almost nothing but. "Only through concentration of a large number of media in a few hands can one attain a true orchestration, a continuity, and an application of scientific methods of influencing individuals." That such concentration is occurring daily, Ellul says, is an established fact, and its results may well be an almost total homogenization of thought among those the media reach. We cannot afford to ignore Norbert Wiener's observation of a paradox that results from our increasing technological capability in electronic communication: as the number of messages increases, the amount of information carried decreases. We have more media to communicate fewer significant ideas.

Still another way of saying this is that, while there has been a tremendous increase in media, there has been, at the same time, a decrease in available and viable "democratic" channels of communication. For example, as a means of affecting public policy, the town meeting is dead. Significant community action (without violence) is increasingly rare. A small printing press in one's home, as an instrument of social change, is absurd. Traditional forms of dissent and protest seem impractical, e.g., letters to the editor, street-corner speeches, etc. No one can reach many people unless he has access to the mass media. As this is written, for example, there is no operational two-way communication possible with respect to United States policies and procedures in Vietnam. The communication is virtually all one way: from the top down, via the mass media, especially TV. The pressure on everyone is to subscribe without question to policies formulated in the Pentagon. The President appears on TV and clearly makes the point that anyone who does not accept "our policy" can be viewed only as lending aid and comfort to the enemy. The position has been elaborately developed in all media that "peaceniks" are failing in the obligation to "support our boys overseas." The effect of this process on all of us is to leave no alternative but to accept policy, act on orders from above, and implement the policy without question or dialogue. This is what Edgar Friedenberg calls "creeping Eichmann-ism," a sort of spiritless, mechanical, abstract functioning which does not allow much room for individual thought and action.

As Paul Goodman has pointed out, there are many forms of censorship, and one of them is to deny access to "loudspeakers" to those with dissident ideas, or even *any* ideas. This is easy to do (and not necessarily conspiratorial) when the loudspeakers are owned and operated by mammoth corporations with enormous investments in their proprietorship. What we get is an entirely new politics, including the possibility that a major requirement for the holding of political office be prior success as a show-business personality. Goodman writes in *Like a Conquered Province*:

> The traditional American sentiment is that a decent society cannot be built by dominant official policy anyway, but only by grassroots resistance, community cooperation, individual enterprise, and citizenly vigilance to protect liberty. . . . *The question is whether or not our beautiful libertarian, pluralist, and populist experiment is viable in modern conditions.* If it's not, I don't know any other acceptable politics, and I am a man without a country.

Is it possible that there are millions becoming men without a country? Men who are increasingly removed from the sources of power? Men who have fewer and fewer ideas available to them, and fewer and fewer ways of expressing themselves meaningfully and effectively? Might the frustration thus engendered be one of the causes of the increasing use of violence as a form of statement?

We come then to a second problem which makes necessary a "subversive" role for the schools. This one may appropriately be called the "Change Revolution." In order to illustrate what this means, we will use the media again and the metaphor of a clock face. Imagine a clock face with sixty minutes on it. Let the clock stand for the time men have had access to writing systems. Our clock would thus represent something like 3,000 years, and each minute on our clock fifty years. On this scale, there were no significant media changes until about nine minutes ago. At that time, the printing press came into use in Western culture. About three minutes ago, the telegraph, photograph, and locomotive arrived. Two minutes ago: the telephone, rotary press, motion pictures, automobile, airplane, and radio. One minute ago, the talking picture. Television has appeared in the last ten seconds, the computer in the last five, and communications satellites in the last second. The laser beam—perhaps the most potent medium of communication of all—appeared only a fraction of a second ago.

It would be possible to place almost any area of life on our clock face and get roughly the same measurements. For example, in medicine, you would have almost no significant changes until about one minute ago. In fact, until one minute ago, as Jerome Frank has said, almost the whole history of medicine is the history of the placebo effect. About a minute ago, antibiotics arrived. About ten seconds ago, open-heart surgery. In fact, within the past ten seconds there probably have been more changes in medicine than is represented by all the rest of the time on our clock. This is what some people call the "knowledge explosion." It is happening in every field of knowledge susceptible to scientific inquiry.

The standard reply to any comment about change (for example, from many educators) is that change isn't new and that it is easy to exaggerate its meaning. To such replies, Norbert Wiener had a useful answer: the difference between a fatal and a therapeutic dose of strychnine is "only a matter of degree." In other words, change isn't new; what is new is the *degree of change.* As our clock-face metaphor was intended to suggest, about three minutes ago there developed a qualitative difference in the character of change. Change changed.

This is really quite a new problem. For example, up until the last generation it was possible to be born, grow up, and spend a life in the United States without moving more than fifty miles from home, without ever confronting serious questions about one's basic values, beliefs, and patterns of behavior. Indeed, without ever confronting serious challenges to anything one knew. Stability and consequent predictability—within "natural cycles"—was the characteristic mode. But now, in just the last minute, we've reached the stage where change occurs so rapidly that each of us in the course of our lives has continuously to work out a set of values, beliefs, and patterns of behavior that are viable, or *seem* viable, to each of us personally. And just when we have identified a workable system, it turns out to be irrelevant because so much has changed while we were doing it.

Of course, this frustrating state of affairs applies to our education as well. If you are over twenty-five years of age, the mathematics you were taught in school is "old"; the grammar you were taught is obsolete and in disrepute; the biology, completely out of date, and the history, open to serious question. The best that can be said of you, assuming that you *remember* most of what you were told and read, is that you are a walking encyclopedia of outdated information. As Alfred North Whitehead pointed out in *The Adventure of Ideas*:

> Our sociological theories, our political philosophy, our practical maxims of business, our political economy, and our doctrines of education are derived from an unbroken tradition of great thinkers and of practical examples from the age of Plato . . . to the end of the last century. The whole of this tradition is warped by the vicious assumption that each generation will substantially live amid the conditions governing the lives of its fathers and will transmit those conditions to mould with equal force the lives of its children. *We are living in the first period of human history for which this assumption is false.*

All of which brings us to the third problem: the "burgeoning bureaucracy." We are brought there because bureaucracies, in spite of their seeming indispensability, are by their nature highly resistant to change. The motto of most bureaucracies is, "Carry On, Regardless." There is an essential mindlessness about them which causes them, in most circumstances, to accelerate entropy rather than to impede it. Bureaucracies rarely ask themselves Why?, but only How? John Gardner, who as President of the Carnegie Corporation and (as of this writing) Secretary of Health, Education, and Welfare has learned about bureaucracies at first hand, has explained them very well:

> To accomplish renewal, we need to understand what prevents it. When we talk about revitalizing a society, we tend to put exclusive emphasis on finding new ideas. But there is usually no shortage of new ideas; the problem is to get a hearing for them. And that means breaking through the crusty rigidity and stubborn complacency of the *status quo*. The aging society develops elaborate defenses against new ideas— "mind-forged manacles," in William Blake's vivid phrase. . . . As a society becomes more concerned with precedent and custom, it comes to care more about how things are done and less about whether they are done. The man who wins acclaim is not the one who "gets things done" but the one who has an ingrained knowledge of the rules and accepted practices. Whether he accomplishes anything is less important than whether he conducts himself in an "appropriate" manner.
>
> The body of custom, convention, and "reputable" standards exercises such an oppressive effect on creative minds that new developments in a field often originate outside the area of respectable practice.

In other words, bureaucracies are the repositories of conventional assumptions and standard practices—two of the greatest accelerators of entropy.

We could put before you a volume of other quotations—from Machiavelli to Paul Goodman—describing how bureaucratic structures retard the development and application of new survival strategies. But in doing so, we would risk creating the impression that we stand with Goodman in yearning for some anarchistic Utopia in which the Army, the Police, General Motors, the U.S. Office of Education, the Post Office, et al. do not exist. We are not "against" bureaucracies, any more than we are "for" them. They are like electric plugs. They will probably not go away, but they do need to be controlled if the prerogatives of a democratic society are to remain visible and usable. This is why we ask that the schools be "subversive," that they serve as a kind of antibureaucracy bureaucracy, providing the young with a "What is it good for?" perspective on its own society. Certainly, it is unrealistic to expect those who control the media to perform that function. Nor the generals and the politicians. Nor is it reasonable to expect the "intellectuals" to do it for they do not have access to the majority of youth. But schoolteachers do, and so the primary responsibility rests with them.

The trouble is that most teachers have the idea that they are in some other sort of business. Some believe, for example, that they are in the "information dissemination" business. This was a reasonable business up to about a minute or two ago on our clock. (But then, so was the horseshoe business and the candle-snuffer business.) The signs that their business is failing are abundant, but they keep at it all the more diligently. Santayana told us that a fanatic is someone who redoubles his efforts when he has forgotten his aim. In this case, even if the aim has not been forgotten, it is simply irrelevant. But the effort has been redoubled anyway.

There are some teachers who think they are in the "transmission of our cultural heritage" business, which is not an unreasonable business if you are concerned with the whole clock and not just its first fifty-seven minutes. The trouble is that most teachers find the last three minutes too distressing to deal with, which is exactly why they are in the wrong business. Their students find the last three minutes distressing—and confusing—too, especially the last thirty seconds, and they need *help*. While they have to live with TV, film, the LP record, communication satellites, and the laser beam, their teachers are still talking as if the only medium on the scene is Gutenberg's printing press. While they have to understand psychology and psychedelics, anthopology and anthropomorphism, birth control and biochemistry, their teachers are teaching "subjects" that mostly don't exist anymore. While they need to find new roles for themselves as social, political, and religious organisms, their teachers (as Edgar Friedenberg has documented so painfully) are acting almost entirely as shills for corporate interests, shaping them up to be functionaries in one bureaucracy or another.

Unless our schools can switch to the right business, their clientele will either go elsewhere (as many are doing) or go into a severe case of "future shock," to use a relatively new phrase. Future shock occurs when you are confronted by the fact that the world you were educated to believe in doesn't exist. Your images of reality are apparitions that disappear on contact. There are several ways of responding to such a condition, one of which is to withdraw and allow oneself to be overcome by a sense of impotence. More commonly, one continues to act *as if* his apparitions were substantial, relentlessly pursuing a course of action that he knows will fail him. You may have noticed that there are scores of political, social, and religious leaders who are clearly suffering from advanced cases of future shock. They repeat over and over again the words that are supposed to represent the world about them. But nothing seems to work out. And then they repeat the words again and again. Alfred Korzybski used a somewhat different metaphor to describe what we have been calling "future shock." He likened one's language to a map. The map is intended to describe the territory that we call "reality," i.e., the world outside of our skins.

When there is a close correspondence between map and territory, there tends to be a high degree of effective functioning, especially where it relates to survival. When there is little correspondence between map and territory, there is a strong tendency for entropy to make substantial gains. In this context, the terrifying question "What did you learn in school today?" assumes immense importance for all of us. We just may not survive another generation of inadvertent entropy helpers. . . . What is the necessary business of the schools? To create eager consumers? To transmit the dead ideas, values, metaphors, and information of three minutes ago? To create smoothly functioning bureaucrats? *These* aims are truly subversive since they undermine our chances of surviving as a viable, democratic society. And they do their work in the name of convention and standard practice. We would like to see the schools go into the antientropy business. Now, that is subversive, too. But the purpose is to subvert attitudes, beliefs, and assumptions that foster chaos and uselessness.

What Is Education?

GEORGE LEONARD

To learn is to change. Education is a process that changes the learner.
Do not blame teachers or their administrators if they fail to educate,
to change their students. For the task of *preventing* the new generation from changing in any deep or significant way is precisely what
most societies require of their educators. Perhaps it is enough that
schools should go on with their essentially conservative function:
passing on the established values and skills of the past. Perhaps schools
should not change but civilize (restrict human behavior) while super-
imposing skills and polish. Who would experiment with children's
lives?

But something is wrong. Every wind-tee we raise into the gales of
the future tells us that people had better find new ways of acting, of
relating, of dealing with their environments. Just to survive, it appears, we need a new human nature; so we find ways of talking about
"the gap between technology and sociology." We sense that our salvation lies in education; so we trifle around the edges of things peda-
gogical and call it "revolution." When nothing much happens, we
turn upon our educators with a harshness that dishonors not them,
but ourselves. We damn them as mere babysitters when this is the
function we most avidly press upon them. We ridicule them for preoccupation with "method" when no really workable methods have
been provided them and, indeed, this is what they most desperately
need. We slander them, slyly, as somehow wanting in the finely honed
intellects of their detractors or, archly, as "lower-middle-class-upward-
mobile," when the ability to score high on those culturally rigged
ratings we call "intelligence tests" has little to do with the ability to
educate and indeed sometimes signifies a doctrinaire, inhuman rigidity
that resists change.

No, educators are not the culprits. They are the valiant slaves of
our society, condemned to perpetuate the very system that victimizes

"What Is Education?" From George Leonard, *Education and Ecstasy* (New York:
Delacorte Press, 1968), pp. 7–21. Copyright © 1968 by George Leonard. Reprinted
by permission of Delacorte Press and The Sterling Lord Agency, Inc.

them. They are sometimes bewildered, sometimes angry, often tired because—at a time of harrowing cultural upheaval, with practically an entire continental civilization's children in school—the mutual deception between them and their masters is wearing thin. If education is a process that causes real change, not just in one's ability to manipulate symbols, but in every aspect of one's being, then what today's educators are called upon to do may be many things, but it is not education. . . .

But no one can be rescued from learning; learning is what human life is. Brain researcher John Lilly and others have tried to cut off the connections between the inner self and the world of the senses from which the stuff of learning comes. In these sensory-deprivation experiments, the subject is suspended, nude, in a tank of tepid water. His eyes are blindfolded, his ears are plugged; he breathes through a face mask. He becomes, as far as possible, a disembodied brain. But the brain is not content to rest. It reshuffles past learning, builds rich new inner worlds in which the self seems to move and learn. "When I went in the tank," Dr. Lilly told me, "I could will myself into the center of a giant computer. I could see the connections reaching out from me in every direction in vivid colors. Or, if I wished, I could ski across the top of the Andes, skimming from one peak to another."

There are no neutral moments. Even in those classrooms where the education some of us might hope for is impossible, a kind of shadowy, negative learning is going on. Some pupils learn how to daydream; others, how to take tests. Some learn the petty deceptions involved in cheating; others, the larger deceptions of playing the school game absolutely straight (the well-kept notebook, the right answer, the senior who majors in good grades). Most learn that the symbolic tricks their keepers attempt to teach them have little to do with their own deeper feelings or anything in the here and now. The activity that masquerades under the ancient and noble name of "education" actually seems to serve as a sort of ransom to the future, a down payment toward "getting ahead"—or at least toward not falling behind. Lifetime-earnings figures are pressed upon potential high-school dropouts. These figures seem to show that giving an acceptable interpretation of "Ode on a Grecian Urn" somehow means you will live in a better suburb and drive a bigger car. A vision of Florida retirement superimposes itself on every diagram in plane geometry. Some students refuse to pay the ransom, and you should not be surprised that these students may be what the society itself calls the "brighter" ones. (According to Dr. Louis Bright, director of research for the U.S. Office of Education, high-school dropouts in large cities where the figures are available have higher IQs than high-school graduates.) But dropouts and graduates alike have had plenty of practice in fragmenting their lives—segregating senses from emotions from intellect, building boxes for art and abstractions, divorcing the self from the reality and the joy of the present moment. No need for obscure psychological explanations for modern man's fragmentation; that is what his schools teach.

Perhaps this has been so ever since education was first formalized. Historian Arnold Toynbee traces the disintegration of the Chinese Empire under the Ts'in and Han Dynasties as well as that of the Roman Empire, in part, to their attempts to extend formal education from the privileged minority to a wider circle. "One reason," Toynbee wrote, "was that the former privileged minority's traditional system of education was impoverished in the process of being disseminated. It degenerated into a formal education in book learning divorced from a spontaneous apprenticeship for life. . . . In fact, the art of playing with words was substituted for the art of living."

In more primitive cultures, the Polynesian, for example, education was sacramental. Every aspect of life, every act of living was related, and life's procedures were learned in a manner simultaneously more intense and more casual than would seem possible in a formal institution. All things were observed and experienced in unity. The educational institutions of Western civilization, on the other hand, have almost always been formalistic and symbolic to the extreme. When the Renaissance academies took the Roman educator Quintilian for their model, they managed to adopt his most negative and stultifying precepts, leading to purely verbal training in ancient literature—even though Quintilian's was a specialized school for orators.

Until relatively recent times, however, only a tiny proportion of the West's population ever saw the inside of an academy. (As recently as 1900, less than 10 percent of American sixteen-year-olds were in school.) Education for the vast majority, though less sacramental and ecstatic, resembled that of the Polynesians. Under the tutelage of such stable institutions as the family, the farm, the village, the church and the craft guild, the ordinary young Westerner served his apprenticeship for living—limiting, perhaps, but all of a piece. As for the aristocrat, he lived and learned under the sure guidance of class tradition and accepted formal education primarily as an instrument for fortifying class lines. Better than badges and plumes were Latin and Greek, maintained, under the fiction of teaching "thinking," for centuries after the world's literature was available in translation. (All attempts to prove that the study of Latin improves thinking skills have failed.) A school accent served as well as a school tie in bolstering those barriers between people which seemed so necessary in building and maintaining a militaristic, colonial empire.

The successive historical events we know as the Enlightenment, the process of democratization, the Industrial Revolution and the explosive developments of consumerism and leisure weakened the prime educating institutions of the past (family, farm, village, church, guild), leaving successively more of the younger generation's total education-for-living to the schools and colleges. The young crowded into classrooms and were led away from life.

Reformers tried to stop the fragmentation. The greatest among them was John Dewey. We have at last reached a hillock in time from which we can look across a lot of pointless controversy and view this man's genius with a certain clarity and dispassion. Dewey sought a unity in life. He recognized that education is a process of living and not a preparation for future living. He believed that education is the fundamental method of social progress and reform. He provided a philosophical underpinning for the Progressive Education movement which, simply stated, saved the American public school system by making it just flexible and forgiving enough to accommodate the children of immigrants, poor farmers and other followers of the American dream.

But Dewey did not provide educators with the hard-honed tools of true reform. Seduced by the psychology of his time, he enjoined teachers to spend more energy helping children form "images" than making them learn certain things. More disabling yet, he was fascinated with the notion of "interests," which he felt would automatically manifest themselves in children when they were *ready* to learn something. This notion, somewhat misinterpreted, led a generation of teachers to wait for children to show signs of "interest" before they moved ahead and thereby woefully to underrate their capacity for learning. Teachers found further justification for just waiting in the work of developmental psychologists who followed Dewey. These good-hearted doubters are still around with stacks of studies to show us precisely what children *cannot* do until this age or that age. Their studies become worthless, as we shall see in the next chapter, when children are placed in learning environments designed to let them crash through all the ceilings erected by the past. Progressive education was a useful, humane and sometimes joyful reform, but it was not the true revolution in education that the times then needed and now demand. The worst of that movement may be summed up in one sentence: It is as cruel to bore a child as to beat him.

Learning eventually involves interaction between learner and environment, and its effectiveness relates to the frequency, variety and intensity of the interaction.

For the most part, the schools have not really changed. They have neither taken up the slack left by the retreat of the past's prime educators nor significantly altered the substance and style of their teaching. The most common mode of instruction today, as in the Renaissance, has a teacher sitting or standing before a number of students in a single room, presenting them with facts and techniques of a verbal-rational nature. Our expectation of what the human animal can learn, can do, can be remains remarkably low and timorous. Our definition of education's root purpose remains shortsightedly utilitarian. Our map of the territory of learning remains antiquated: vocational training, homemaking, driving and other "fringe" subjects, themselves limiting and fragmenting, have invaded the curriculum, but are generally considered outside the central domain of "education." This domain, this venerable bastion, is still a place where people are trained to split their world into separate symbolic systems, the better to cope with and manipulate it. Such "education," suprarationalistic and analytical to the extreme, has made possible colonialism, the production line, space voyaging and the H-bomb. But it has not made people happy or whole, nor does it now offer them ways to change, deep down, in an age that cries out with the urgency of a rocket's flight, "Change or die."

All that goes on in most schools and colleges today is only a thin slice, as we shall see, of what education can become. And yet, our present institutions show a maddening inefficiency even in dealing with this thin slice. In recent years, there has been a small net gain in American students' performance in the basic subjects. But this has been accomplished only at the cost of a large increase in gross effort—more and more homework assigned under threat of more and tougher exams to force students to learn, on their own, what most of today's teachers have long since realized they cannot teach them. A visitor from another planet might conclude that our schools are hell-bent on creating—in a society that offers leisure and demands creativity—a generation of joyless drudges.

There are signs the school will not succeed in this drab mission. Already, the seeds of a real change are germinating—on college campuses, in teachers' associations, in laboratories of science, in out-of-the-way places. . . . This reform would bypass entirely the patchwork remedial measures (Spanish in second grade, teachers in teams, subject matter updated) that presently pass for reform. It cuts straight to the heart of the educational enterprise, in and out of school, seeking new method, content, idiom, domain, purpose and, indeed, a new definition of education. Far from decrying and opposing an onrushing technology, it sees technology as an ally, a force that can as easily enhance as diminish the human spirit. Avoiding hard-and-fast assumptions of its own, it is rigorous in questioning some of the automatic assumptions of the past. It is a new journey. To join it, you had best leave your awe of history behind, open your mind to unfamiliar or even disreputable solutions if they are the ones that work, look upon all systems of abstractions as strictly tentative and throw out of the window every prior guideline about what human beings can accomplish.

The prospects are exhilarating, though it is becoming dangerous to write about them if only because nowadays it is so hard to stay ahead of reality. Let us assume the future will surprise us; and, so assuming, speculate only about what is already coming to pass. For example, the following prospects are in the realm of possibility:

> Ways can be worked out to help average students learn whatever is needed of present-day subject matter in a third or less of the present time, pleasurably rather than painfully, with almost certain success. Better yet, the whole superstructure of rational-symbolic knowledge can be rearranged so that these aspects of life's possibilities can be perceived and learned as unity and diversity within change rather than fragmentation within an illusory permanence.

> Ways can be worked out to provide a new apprenticeship for living, appropriate to a technological age of constant change. Many new types of learning having to do with crucial areas of human functioning that are now neglected or completely ignored can be made a part of the educational enterprise. Much of what will be learned tomorrow does not today have even a commonly accepted name.

> Ways can be worked out so that almost every day will be a "teachable day," so that almost every educator can share with his students the inspired moments of learning now enjoyed by only the most rare and remarkable.

> Education in a new and greatly broadened sense can become a lifelong pursuit for everyone. To go on learning, to go on sharing that learning with others may well be considered a purpose worthy of mankind's ever-expanding capacities.

Education, at best, is ecstatic.

If education in the coming age is to be, not just a part of life, but the main purpose of life, then education's purpose will, at last, be viewed as central. What, then, is the purpose, the goal of education? A large part of the answer may well be what men of this civilization have longest feared and most desired: *the achievement of moments of ecstasy.* Not fun, not simply pleasure as in the equation of Bentham and Mill, not the libido pleasure of Freud, but ecstasy, *ananda,* the ultimate delight.

Western civilization, for well-known historical reasons, has traditionally eschewed ecstasy as a threat to goal-oriented control of men, matter and energy—and has suffered massive human unhappiness. Other civilizations, notably that of India, have turned their best energies toward the attainment of ecstasy, while neglecting practical goals —and have suffered massive human unhappiness. Now modern science and technology seem to be preparing a situation where the successful control of practical matters and the attainment of ecstasy can safely coexist; where each reinforces the other; and, quite possibly, where neither can long exist *without* the other. Abundance and population control already are logically and technologically feasible. At the same time, cybernation, pervasive and instantaneous communication and other feedback devices of increasing speed, range and sensitivity extend and enhance man's sensory apparatus, multiplying the possibilities for understanding and ecstasy as well as for misunderstanding and destruction. The times demand that we choose delight.

Do discipline and mastery of technique stand in opposition to freedom, self-expression and the ecstatic moment? Most Western educators have acted as if they did. Strange, when there exist so many models of the marriage between the two. Take the artistic endeavor: the composer discovers that the soul of creation transcends the body of form only when form is his completely. The violinist arrives at the sublime only through utter mastery of technique. The instruments of living that are now coming into our hands—rich, responsive and diverse—require mastery. The process of mastery itself can be ecstatic, leading to delight that transcends mastery.

The new revolutionaries of education must soothe those who fear techniques no less than those who fear delight. Many a liberal educational reform has foundered on lack of specific tools for accomplishing its purposes—even if a tool may be something as simple as knowing *precisely when* to leave the learner entirely alone. Education must use its most powerful servant, technique, in teaching skills that go far beyond those which submit to academic achievement tests. Even today, as will be seen, specific, systematic ways are being worked out to help people learn to love, to feel deeply, to expand their inner selves, to create, to enter new realms of being.

What is education? The answer may be far simpler than we imagine. Matters of great moment and processes that affect our lives at the very heart are generally less obscure and mysterious than they at first appear. The travels of celestial bodies, once requiring the efforts of a pantheon of gods, now follow a few easy formulas. Chemical reactions explained by essences, vapors, phlogiston became easier to understand when reduced to a single variable: weight. Mankind's most awesome mystery, fire, once understood, could be handled by little children. Throughout history, the way to understanding, control and ecstasy has been a long, sinuous journey toward simplicity and unity.

To learn is to change. Education is a process that changes the learner.
The first part of a simple, operational definition of education calls on the educator to view his work as consequential, not theoretical or formalistic. Looking for *change* in his student (and himself) as a measure, he will discover what is important in his work and what is waste motion. Asking himself, "What has changed in the student, and me, because of this particular experience?," he may have to answer that what has changed is only the student's ability to recite a few more

"facts" than he could before the session. He may find that the student has changed in wider and deeper ways. He may have to admit that the student has hardly changed at all or, if so, in a way that no one had intended. In any case, he will not ask himself the *wrong* questions ("Wasn't my presentation brilliant?" "Why are they so dumb?").

Looking for the *direction and further consequences* of the change, he will be forced to ask whether it is for the good of the student, himself and society. In doing this, the educator will discover he has to become sensitive to what is happening to the student at every moment, and thereby will become a feeling participant in the circle of learning. Viewing learning as anything that changes the learner's behavior, the educator will expand his domain a thousandfold, for he will realize that there are hardly any aspects of human life that cannot be changed, educated. He will see clearly that, if the educational enterprise limits itself to what is now ordinarily taught in classrooms, it will be pursuing failure in the coming age.

Learning involves interaction between the learner and his environment, and its effectiveness relates to the frequency, variety and intensity of the interaction.

Guided by this second part of the definition, the educator will pay far closer attention to the learning environment than ever before in education's history. The environment may be a book, a game, a programmed device, a choir, a brainwave feedback mechanism, a silent room, an interactive group of students, even a teacher—but in every case, the educator will turn his attention from mere *presentation* of the environment (a classroom lecture, for example) to the *response* of the learner. He will study and experiment with the learning process, the series of responses, at every step along the way, better to utilize the increasing capacities of environment and learner as each changes. Observing the work of what have been called "master teachers" in this light, he will find that their mysterious, unfathomable "artistry" actually comprises a heightened sensitivity to student responses plus the use of personally developed, specific, flexible techniques. The educator will work out ways to help every teacher become an "artist."

Education, at best, is ecstatic.

The first two parts of the definition need the third, which may be seen as a way of praising learning for its own sake. And yet, it goes further, for the educator of the coming age will not be vague or theoretical about this matter. As he loses his fear of delight, he will become explicit and specific in his pursuit of the ecstatic moment. At its best, its most effective, its most unfettered, the moment of learning is a moment of delight. This essential and obvious truth is demonstrated for us every day by the baby and the preschool child, by the class of the "artist" teacher, by learners of all ages interacting with new learning programs that are designed for success. When joy is absent, the effectiveness of the learning process falls and falls until the human being is operating hesitantly, grudgingly, fearfully at only a tiny fraction of his potential.

The notion that ecstasy is mainly an inward-directed experience testifies to our distrust of our own society, of the outer environment we have created for ourselves. Actually, the varieties of ecstasy are limitless. . . . The new educator will seek out the possibility of delight in every form of learning. He will realize that solving an elegant mathematical problem and making love are different classes in the same order of things, sharing common ecstasy. He will find that even education now considered nothing more than present drudgery for future payoff—learning the multiplication tables, for example—can become joyful when a skillfully designed learning environment (a programmed game, perhaps) makes the learning quick and easy. Indeed, the skillful pursuit of ecstasy will make the pursuit of excellence, not for the few, but for the many, what it never has been—successful. And yet, make no mistake about it, excellence, as we speak of it today, will be only a by-product of a greater unity, a deeper delight.

Persons and Experience

R. D. LAING

INTERPERSONAL EXPERIENCE AND BEHAVIOR

Our task is both to experience and to conceive the concrete, that is to
say, reality in its fullness and wholeness.

But this is quite impossible, immediately. Experientially and con-
ceptually, we have fragments.

We begin from concepts of the single person, from the relations between two or more persons, from groups or from society at large; or
from the material world, and conceive of individuals as secondary. We
can derive the main determinants of our individual and social behavior from external exigencies. All these views are partial vistas and
partial concepts. Theoretically we need a spiral of expanding and con-
tracting schemata that enable us to move freely and without discon-
tinuity from varying degrees of abstraction to greater or lesser degrees
of concreteness. Theory is the articulated vision of experience. . . .

Can human beings be persons today? Can a man be his actual self
with another man or woman? Before we can ask such an optimistic
question as, "What is a personal relationship?," we have to ask if a
personal relationship is possible, or, *are persons possible* in our present
situation? We are concerned with the possibility of man. This question
can be asked only through its facets. Is love possible? Is freedom possible?

Whether or not all, or some, or no human beings are persons, I wish
to define a person in a twofold way: in terms of experience, as a center
of orientation of the objective universe; and in terms of behavior, as
the origin of actions. Personal experience transforms a given field onto
a field of intention and action: only through action can our experience
be transformed. It is tempting and facile to regard "persons" as only
separate objects in space, who can be studied as any other natural
objects can be studied. But just as Kierkegaard remarked that one will

never find consciousness by looking down a microscope at brain cells or anything else, so one will never find persons by studying persons as though they were only objects. A person is the me or you, he or she, whereby an object is experienced. Are these centers of experience and origins of actions living in entirely unrelated worlds of their own composition? Everyone must refer here to their own experience. My own experience as a center of experience and origin of action tells me that this is not so. My experience and my action occur in a social field of reciprocal influence and interaction. I experience myself, identifiable as Ronald Laing by myself and others, as experienced by and acted upon by others, who refer to that person I call "me" as "you" or "him," or grouped together as "one of us" or "one of them" or "one of you."

This feature of personal relations does not arise in the correlation of the behavior of nonpersonal objects. Many social scientists deal with their embarrassment by denying its occasion. Nevertheless, the natural scientific world is complicated by the presence of certain identifiable entities, reidentifiable reliably over periods of years, whose behavior is either the manifestation or a concealment of a view of the world equivalent in ontological status to that of the scientist.

People may be observed to sleep, eat, walk, talk, etc. in relatively predictable ways. We must not be content with observation of this kind alone. Observation of behavior must be extended by inference to attributions about experience. Only when we can begin to do this can we really construct the experiential-behavioral system that is the human species.

It is quite possible to study the visible, audible, smellable effulgences of human bodies, and much study of human behavior has been in those terms. One can lump together very large numbers of units of behavior and regard them as a statistical population, in no way different from the multiplicity constituting a system of nonhuman objects. But one will not be studying persons. In a science of persons, I shall state as axiomatic that: behavior is a function of experience; and both experience and behavior are always in relation to someone or something other than self.

When two (or more) persons are in relation, the behavior of each towards the other is mediated by the experience by each of the other, and the experience of each is mediated by the behavior of each. There is no contiguity between the behavior of one person and that of the other. Much human behavior can be seen as a unilateral or bilateral *attempt* to eliminate experience. A person may treat another *as though* he were not a person, and he may act himself *as though* he were not a person. There is no contiguity between one person's experience and another's. My experience of you is always mediated through your *behavior*. Behavior that is the direct consequence of impact, as of one billiard ball hitting another, or experience directly transmitted to experience, as in the possible cases of extrasensory perception, is not personal.

NORMAL ALIENATION FROM EXPERIENCE

The relevance of Freud to our time is largely his insight and, to a very considerable extent, his *demonstration* that the *ordinary* person is a shriveled, desiccated fragment of what a person can be.

As adults, we have forgotten most of our childhood, not only its contents but its flavor; as men of the world, we hardly know of the existence of the inner world: we barely remember our dreams, and make little sense of them when we do; as for our bodies, we retain just sufficient proprioceptive sensations to coordinate our movements and to ensure the minimal requirements for biosocial survival—to register fatigue, signals for food, sex, defecation, sleep; beyond that, little or nothing. Our capacity to think, except in the service of what we are dangerously deluded in supposing is our self-interest and in conformity with common sense, is pitifully limited: our capacity even to see, hear, touch, taste and smell is so shrouded in veils of mystification that an intensive discipline of unlearning is necessary for *anyone* before one can begin to experience the world afresh, with innocence, truth and love.

And immediate experience of, in contrast to belief or faith in, a spiritual realm of demons, spirits, Powers, Dominions, Principalities, Seraphim and Cherubim, the Light, is even more remote. As domains of experience become more alien to us, we need greater and greater open-mindedness even to conceive of their existence.

Many of us do not know, or even believe, that every night we enter zones of reality in which we forget our waking life as regularly as we forget our dreams when we awake. Not all psychologists know of fantasy as a modality of experience, and the, as it were, contrapuntal interweaving of different experiential modes. Many who are aware of fantasy believe that fantasy is the farthest that experience goes under "normal" circumstances. Beyond that are simply "pathological" zones of hallucinations, phantasmagoric mirages, delusions.

This state of affairs represents an almost unbelievable devastation of our experience. Then there is empty chatter about maturity, love, joy, peace.

This is itself a consequence of and further occasion for the divorce of our experience, such as is left of it, from our behavior.

What we call "normal" is a product of repression, denial, splitting, projection, introjection and other forms of destructive action on experience (see below). It is radically estranged from the structure of being.

The more one sees this, the more senseless it is to continue with generalized descriptions of supposedly specifically schizoid, schizophrenic, hysterical "mechanisms."

There are forms of alienation that are relatively strange to statistically "normal" forms of alienation. The "normally" alienated person, by reason of the fact that he acts more or less like everyone else, is taken to be sane. Other forms of alienation that are out of step with the prevailing state of alienation are those that are labeled by the "normal" majority as bad or mad.

The condition of alienation, of being asleep, of being unconscious, of being out of one's mind, is the condition of the normal man.

Society highly values its normal man. It educates children to lose themselves and to become absurd, and thus to be normal.

Normal men have killed perhaps 100,000,000 of their fellow normal men in the last fifty years.

Our behavior is a function of our experience. We act according to the way we see things.

If our experience is destroyed, our behavior will be destructive.

If our experience is destroyed, we have lost our own selves.

How much human *behavior*, whether the interactions between persons themselves or between groups and groups, is intelligible in terms of human *experience*? Either our interhuman behavior is unintelligible, in that we are simply the passive vehicles of inhuman processes whose ends are as obscure as they are at present outside our control, or our own behavior towards each other is a function of our own experience and our own intentions, however alienated we are from them. In the latter case, we must take final responsibility for what we make of what we are made of.

We will find no intelligibility in behavior if we see it as an inessential phase in an essentially inhuman process. We have had accounts of men as animals, men as machines, men as biochemical complexes with certain ways of their own, but there remains the greatest difficulty in achieving a human understanding of man in human terms.

Men at all times have been subject, as they believed or experienced, to forces from the stars, from the gods, or to forces that now blow through society itself, appearing as the stars once did to determine human fate.

Men have, however, always been weighed down not only by their sense of subordination to fate and chance, to ordained external necessities or contingencies, but by a sense that their very own thoughts and feelings, in their most intimate interstices, are the outcome, the resultant, of processes which they undergo.

A man can estrange himself from himself by mystifying himself and others. He can also have what he does stolen from him by the agency of others.

If we are stripped of experience, we are stripped of our deeds; and if our deeds are, so to speak, taken out of our hands like toys from the hands of children, we are bereft of our humanity. We cannot be deceived. Men can and do destroy the humanity of other men, and the condition of this possibility is that we are interdependent. We are not self-contained monads producing no effects on each other except our reflections. We are both acted upon, changed for good or ill, by other men; and we are agents who act upon others to affect them in different ways. Each of us is the other to the others. Man is a patient-agent, agent-patient, interexperiencing and interacting with his fellows.

It is quite certain that unless we can regulate our behavior much more satisfactorily than at present, then we are going to exterminate ourselves. But as we experience the world, so we act, and this principle holds even when action conceals rather than discloses our experience.

We are not able even to *think* adequately about the behavior that is at the annihilating edge. But what we think is less than what we know; what we know is less than what we love; what we love is so much less than what there is. And to that precise extent we are so much less than what we are.

Yet if nothing else, each time a new baby is born there is a possibility of reprieve. Each child is a new being, a potential prophet, a new spiritual prince, a new spark of light precipitated into the outer darkness. Who are we to decide that it is hopeless?

FANTASY AS A MODE OF EXPERIENCE

The "surface" experience of self and other emerges from a less differentiated experiential matrix. Ontogenetically the very early experiential schemata are unstable and are surmounted, but never entirely. To a greater or lesser extent, the first ways in which the world has made sense to us continue to underpin our whole subsequent experience and actions. Our first way of experiencing the world is largely what psychoanalysts have called fantasy. This modality has its own validity, its own rationality. Infantile fantasy may become a closed enclave, a dissociated undeveloped "unconscious," but this need not be so. This eventuality is another form of alienation. Fantasy as encountered in many people today is split off from what the person regards as his mature, sane, rational, adult experience. We do not then see fantasy in its true function but experienced merely as an intrusive, sabotaging infantile nuisance.

For most of our social life, we largely gloss over this underlying fantasy level of our relationship.

Fantasy is a particular way of relating to the world. It is part of, sometimes the essential part of, the meaning or sense . . . implicit in action. As relationship we may be dissociated from it; as meaning we may not grasp it; as experience it may escape our notice in different ways. That is, it is possible to speak of fantasy being "unconscious," if this general statement is always given specific connotations.

However, although fantasy can be unconscious—that is, although we may be unaware of experience in this mode, or refuse to admit that our behavior implies an experiential relationship or a relational experience that gives it a meaning, often apparent to others if not to ourselves—fantasy need not be thus split from us, whether in terms of its content or modality.

Fantasy, in short, as I am using the term, is always experiential and meaningful; and, if the person is not dissociated from it, relational in a valid way.

Two people sit talking. The one (Peter) is making a point to the other (Paul). He puts his point of view in different ways to Paul for some time, but Paul does not understand.

Let us *imagine* what may be going on, in the sense that I mean by fantasy. Peter is trying to get through to Paul. He feels that Paul is being needlessly closed up against him. It becomes increasingly important to him to soften or get into Paul. But Paul seems hard, impervious and cold. Peter feels he is beating his head against a brick wall. He feels tired, hopeless, progressively more empty as he sees he is failing. Finally he gives up.

Paul feels, on the other hand, that Peter is pressing too hard. He feels he has to fight him off. He doesn't understand what Peter is saying but feels that he has to defend himself from an assault.

The dissociation of each from his fantasy, and the fantasy of the other, betokens the lack of relationship of each to himself and each to the other. They are both more and less related to each other "in fantasy" than each pretends to be to himself and the other.

Here, two roughly complementary fantasy experiences wildly belie the calm manner in which two men talk to each other, comfortably ensconced in their armchairs.

It is mistaken to regard the above description as merely metaphorical.

THE NEGATION OF EXPERIENCE

The physical environment unremittingly offers us possibilities of experience, or curtails them. The fundamental human significance of architecture stems from this. The glory of Athens, as Pericles so lucidly stated, and the horror of so many features of the modern megalopolis is that the former enhanced and the latter constricts man's consciousness.

Here, however, I am concentrating upon what we do to ourselves and to each other.

Let us take the simplest possible interpersonal scheme. Consider Jack and Jill in relation. Then Jack's behavior towards Jill is experienced by Jill in particular ways. How she experiences him affects considerably how she behaves towards him. How she behaves towards him influences (without by any means totally determining) how he experiences her. And his experience of her contributes to his way of behaving towards her, which in turn . . . etc.

Each person may take two fundamentally distinguishable forms of action in this interpersonal system. Each may act on his own experience or upon the other person's experience, *and there is no other form of personal action possible within this system*. That is to say, as long as we are considering personal action of self to self or self to other, the only way one can ever act is on one's own experience or on the other's experience.

Personal action can either open out possibilities of enriched experience or it can shut off possibilities. Personal action is either predominantly validating, confirming, encouraging, supportive, enhancing, or it is invalidating, denying, discouraging, undermining and constricting. It can be creative or destructive.

In a world where the normal condition is one of alienation, most personal action must be destructive both of one's own experience and of that of the other. I shall outline here some of the ways this can be done. I leave the reader to consider from his own experience how pervasive these kinds of action are.

Under the heading of "defense mechanisms," psychoanalysis describes a number of ways in which a person becomes alienated from himself. For example, repression, denial, splitting, projection, introjection. These "mechanisms" are often described in psychoanalytic terms as themselves "unconscious," that is, the person himself appears to be unaware that he is doing this to himself. Even when a person develops sufficient insight to see that "splitting," for example, is going on, he usually experiences this splitting as indeed a mechanism, an impersonal process, so to speak, which has taken over and which he can observe but cannot control or stop.

There is thus some phenomenological validity referring to such "defenses" by the term "mechanism." But we must not stop there. They have this mechanical quality because the person as he experiences himself is dissociated from them. He appears to himself and to others to suffer from them. They seem to be processes he undergoes, and as such he experiences himself as a patient, with a particular psychopathology.

But this is so only from the perspective of his own alienated experience. As he becomes dealienated he is able first of all to become aware of them, if he has not already done so, and then to take the second, even more crucial, step of progressively realizing that these are things he does or has done to himself. Process becomes converted back to praxis, the patient becomes an agent.

Ultimately it is possible to regain the ground that has been lost. These defense mechanisms are actions taken by the person on his own experience. On top of this he has dissociated himself from his own action. The end product of this twofold violence is a person who no longer experiences himself fully as a person, but as a part of a person, invaded by destructive psychopathological "mechanisms" in the face of which he is a relatively helpless victim.

These "defenses" are action on oneself. But "defenses" are not only intrapersonal, they are *transpersonal*. I act not only on myself, I can act upon you. And you act not only on yourself, you act upon me. In each case, an *experience*.

If Jack succeeds in forgetting something, this is of little use if Jill continues to remind him of it. He must induce her not to do so. The safest way would be not just to make her keep quiet about it, but to induce her to forget it also.

Jack may act upon Jill in many ways. He may make her feel guilty for keeping on "bringing it up." He may *invalidate* her experience. This can be done more or less radically. He can indicate merely that it is unimportant or trivial, whereas it is important and significant to her. Going further, he can shift the *modality* of her experience from memory to imagination: "It's all in your imagination." Further still, he can invalidate the *content:* "It never happened that way." Finally, he can invalidate not only the significance, modality and content, but her very capacity to remember at all, and make her feel guilty for doing so into the bargain.

This is not unusual. People are doing such things to each other all the time. In order for such transpersonal invalidation to work, however, it is advisable to overlay it with a thick patina of mystification. For instance, by denying that this is what one is doing, and further invalidating any perception that it is being done by ascriptions such as "How can you think such a thing?" "You must be paranoid." And so on.

§ THE CONCEPT of AFFIRMATIVE EDUCATION

Present classroom practices reveal as one of the major premises of contemporary education the notion that the student begins in ignorance and must receive schooling if he is to be able to survive and function in the world. As Ivan Illich points out later in this book, even the word "education" comes from the medieval methods of turning, or as the alchemists put it, "torturing," an impure substance into a pure one. It is this premise that John Holt is reacting against when he cautions us that "nobody starts off stupid," yet it is the assumed stupidity, vacuity, or ignorance of the young learner that accounts for the forms of educational experience today. A child is said to be bright if he is able to absorb facts; that is, brightness is a measure of how fast he learns. But it is never said that a child is bright and that schooling may be unnecessary or even a hindrance to what he already knows.

The acceptance of this premise has lead to what Chilean educator Paulo Freire, in his searing and profound analysis of the value structure underlying contemporary education, calls "the banking concept" of education. Freire's essay outlines present practice and concludes with a description of the philosophy and the practices that he feels must be adopted. His argument for "problem-posing" education is a cornerstone for the concept of affirmative education. He describes an experiential method that, if applied properly, negates schooling and makes education an opportunity for genuine learning through interaction with life. Freire is committed to affirmative education, which he calls liberating education. Like many of the contributors to this volume, he writes passionately and with conviction about the desperate need for newer, more humane educational practices. This is particularly important because Freire's influence is greater in Latin America, where the educational system, being less developed than that of the United States, is more susceptible to change.

From a very different part of the world comes the contribution of M. V. C. Jeffreys, a highly respected British educator, who argues for an education of feeling. Both Freire and Jeffreys present implementable concepts. To counter the prevailing tendency to turn students into mere IQ scores, Jeffreys presents a theory and possible practical applications that are designed to encourage the fullest emotional growth and that pay due respect to the part of the human psyche responsible for feelings and sensitivities, which are now excluded from the schooling experience. Combining psychoanalytical insights gleaned from fifty years of research into the human personality with an understanding of the nature of creativity, Jeffreys patently dismisses the present distinction between thought and feeling and seeks a more holistic educational experience designed to insure personal growth. In so doing, he offers a vision of affirmative education in which Holt's indictment of dishonesty and the saddening descriptions in the Carnegie Study no longer hold true.

Implicit in the essays by both Freire and Jeffreys is a redefinition of the word *teacher*. The teacher is no longer the storehouse of knowledge so often solicited by the so-called "better" schools. Instead, he or she is someone who is sensitive to growth and who can be an accomplice in personal development. The first requirement is that a teacher be a fully developed and healthy human being, unthreatened by another's creativity, capable of authentic emotional encounters with students, and willing to forgo impressing a captive audience with the fruits of his or her own educational investment.

The nature of the encounter between teacher and student is the subject of Carl Rogers' essay. In this chapter from *Freedom to Learn*, Rogers defines and illustrates the qualities needed in the teacher who applies affirmative educational methods. Rogers draws on psychotherapy, educational philosophy, and case studies to describe the kind of teacher who can be of positive benefit to students. In place of instruction, the didactic transmission of information, Rogers suggests we think of the ability to facilitate learning as the most desirable quality in a teacher.

I have chosen to end this discussion of the concept of affirmative education with a "debate" of sorts. Though Jerome Bruner and George Dennison have not, to my knowledge, ever squared off in public, much can be learned from a direct comparison of their points of view, especially since Dennison specifically takes Bruner to task.

Jerome Bruner is one of the most influential educational psychologists. Like many of the newer critics of educational practice—Kozol, Holt, and others—Dennison, having helped create an educational experience, has felt the need to write about what he learned by actively participating in affirmative education. Whereas Bruner is the theorist and social scientist, Dennison presents himself as a transmitter of what has been learned by *doing and thinking*. This particular distinction already suggests where they will part company. While Bruner is concerned with improving schools, perfecting educational structures, Dennison's commitment is toward improving the quality and nature of young people's educational experience, and this often requires that he oppose and not help perfect what educational institutions do.

Although the two have in common the improvement of educational practice, their substantive disagreement over how this may be accomplished raises many of the issues that frequently undermine the individual teacher and create chaos within the school system. Their debate is and will continue to be carried on throughout the school systems of America and, for this reason, deserves careful attention.

Pedagogy of the Oppressed

PAULO FREIRE

A careful analysis of the teacher-student relationship at any level, inside or outside the school, reveals its fundamentally *narrative* character. This relationship involves a narrating subject (the teacher) and patient, listening objects (the students). The contents, whether values or empirical dimensions of reality, tend in the process of being narrated to become lifeless and petrified. Education is suffering from narration sickness.

The teacher talks about reality as if it were motionless, static, compartmentalized, and predictable. Or else he expounds on a topic completely alien to the existential experience of the students. His task is to "fill" the students with the contents of his narration—contents which are detached from reality, disconnected from the totality that engendered them and could give them significance. Words are emptied of their concreteness and become a hollow, alienated, and alienating verbosity.

The outstanding characteristic of this narrative education, then, is the sonority of words, not their transforming power. "Four times four is sixteen; the capital of Pará is Belém." The student records, memorizes, and repeats these phrases without perceiving what four times four really means, or realizing the true significance of "capital" in the affirmation "the capital of Pará is Belém," that is, what Belém means for Pará and what Pará means for Brazil.

Narration (with the teacher as narrator) leads the students to memorize mechanically the narrated content. Worse yet, it turns them into "containers," into "receptacles" to be "filled" by the teacher. The more completely he fills the receptacles, the better a teacher he is. The more meekly the receptacles permit themselves to be filled, the better students they are.

Education thus becomes an act of depositing, in which the students are the depositories and the teacher is the depositor. Instead of communicating, the teacher issues communiqués and makes deposits which the students patiently receive, memorize, and repeat. This is the "banking" concept of education, in which the scope of action allowed to the students extends only as far as receiving, filing, and storing the deposits. They do, it is true, have the opportunity to become collectors or cataloguers of the things they store. But in the last analysis, it is men themselves who are filed away through the lack of creativity, transformation, and knowledge in this (at best) misguided system. For apart from inquiry, apart from the praxis, men cannot be truly human. Knowledge emerges only through invention and reinvention, through the restless, impatient, continuing, hopeful inquiry men pursue in the world, with the world, and with each other.

In the banking concept of education, knowledge is a gift bestowed by those who consider themselves knowledgeable upon those whom they consider to know nothing. Projecting an absolute ignorance onto others, a characteristic of the ideology of oppression, negates education and knowledge as processes of inquiry. The teacher presents himself to his students as their necessary opposite; by considering their ignorance absolute, he justifies his own existence. The students, alienated like the slave in the Hegelian dialectic, accept their ignorance as justifying the teacher's existence—but, unlike the slave, they never discover that they educate the teacher.

The *raison d'être* of libertarian education, on the other hand, lies in its drive towards reconciliation. Education must begin with the solution of the teacher-student contradiction, by reconciling the poles of the contradiction so that both are simultaneously teachers *and* students.

This solution is not (nor can it be) found in the banking concept. On the contrary, banking education maintains and even stimulates the contradiction through the following attitudes and practices, which mirror oppressive society as a whole:

1. The teacher teaches and the students are taught.
2. The teacher knows everything and the students know nothing.
3. The teacher thinks and the students are thought about.
4. The teacher talks and the students listen—meekly.
5. The teacher disciplines and the students are disciplined.
6. The teacher chooses and enforces his choice, and the students comply.
7. The teacher acts and the students have the illusion of acting through the action of the teacher.
8. The teacher chooses the program content, and the students (who were not consulted) adapt to it.
9. The teacher confuses the authority of knowledge with his own professional authority, which he sets in opposition to the freedom of the students.

10. The teacher is the subject of the learning process, while the pupils are mere objects.

It is not surprising that the banking concept of education regards men as adaptable, manageable beings. The more students work at storing the deposits entrusted to them, the less they develop the critical consciousness which would result from their intervention in the world as transformers of that world. The more completely they accept the passive role imposed on them, the more they tend simply to adapt to the world as it is and to the fragmented view of reality deposited in them.

The capability of banking education to minimize or annul the students' creative power and to stimulate their credulity serves the interests of the oppressors, who care neither to have the world revealed nor to see it transformed. The oppressors use their "humanitarianism" to preserve a profitable situation. Thus they react almost instinctively against any experiment in education which stimulates the critical faculties and is not content with a partial view of reality but always seeks out the ties which link one point to another and one problem to another.

Indeed, the interests of the oppressors lie in "changing the consciousness of the oppressed, not the situation which oppresses them";[1] for the more the oppressed can be led to adapt to that situation, the more easily they can be dominated. To achieve this end, the oppressors use the banking concept of education in conjunction with a paternalistic social action apparatus, within which the oppressed receive the euphemistic title of "welfare recipients." They are treated as individual cases, as marginal men who deviate from the general configuration of a "good, organized, and just" society. The oppressed are regarded as the pathology of the healthy society, which must therefore adjust these "incompetent and lazy" folk to its own patterns by changing their mentality. These marginals need to be "integrated," "incorporated" into the healthy society that they have "forsaken."

The truth is, however, that the oppressed are not "marginals," are not men living "outside" society. They have always been "inside"—inside the structure which made them "beings for others." The solution is not to "integrate" them into the structure of oppression, but to transform that structure so that they can become "beings for themselves." Such transformation, of course, would undermine the oppressors' purposes; hence their utilization of the banking concept of education to avoid the threat of student *conscientização*. . . .

Implicit in the banking concept is the assumption of a dichotomy between man and the world; man is merely *in* the world, not *with* the world or with others; man is spectator, not re-creator. In this view, man is not a conscious being (*corpo consciente*); he is rather the pos-

1. Simone de Beauvoir, *La Pensée de Droite, Aujourd'hui* (Paris).

sessor of *a* consciousness: an empty "mind" passively open to the reception of deposits of reality from the world outside. For example, my desk, my books, my coffee cup, all the objects before me—as bits of the world which surrounds me—would be "inside" me, exactly as I am inside my study right now. This view makes no distinction between being accessible to consciousness and entering consciousness. The distinction, however, is essential: the objects which surround me are simply accessible to my consciousness, not located within it. I am aware of them, but they are not inside me.

It follows logically from the banking notion of consciousness that the educator's role is to regulate the way the world "enters into" the students. His task is to organize a process which already occurs spontaneously, to "fill" the students by making deposits of information which he considers to constitute true knowledge.[2] And since men "receive" the world as passive entities, education should make them more passive still, and adapt them to the world. The educated man is the adapted man, because he is better "fit" for the world. . . .

Yet only through communication can human life hold meaning. The teacher's thinking is authenticated only by the authenticity of the students' thinking. The teacher cannot think for his students, nor can he impose his thought on them. Authentic thinking, thinking that is concerned about *reality*, does not take place in ivory tower isolation, but only in communication. If it is true that thought has meaning only when generated by action upon the world, the subordination of students to teachers becomes impossible.

Because banking education begins with a false understanding of men as objects, it cannot promote the development of what Fromm calls "biophily," but instead produces its opposite: "necrophily":

> While life is characterized by growth in a structured, functional manner, the necrophilous person loves all that does not grow, all that is mechanical. The necrophilous person is driven by the desire to transform the organic into the inorganic, to approach life mechanically, as if all living persons were things. . . . Memory, rather than experience; having, rather than being, is what counts. The necrophilous person can relate to an object—a flower or a person—only if he possesses it; hence a threat to his possession is a threat to himself; if he loses possession he loses contact with the world. . . . He loves control, and in the act of controlling he kills life.[3]

Oppression—overwhelming control—is necrophilic; it is nourished by love of death, not life. The banking concept of education, which

2. This concept corresponds to what Sartre calls the "digestive" or "nutritive" concept of education, in which knowledge is "fed" by the teacher to the students to "fill them out." See Jean-Paul Sartre, "Une idée fondamentale de la phénoménologie de Husserl: L'intentionalité," *Situations I* (Paris, 1947).

3. Eric Fromm, *The Heart of Man* (New York, 1966).

serves the interests of oppression, is also necrophilic. Based on a mechanistic, static, naturalistic, spatialized view of consciousness, it transforms students into receiving objects. It attempts to control thinking and action, leads men to adjust to the world, and inhibits their creative power.

When their efforts to act responsibly are frustrated, when they find themselves unable to use their faculties, men suffer. "This suffering due to impotence is rooted in the very fact that the human equilibrium has been disturbed." [4] But the inability to act which causes men's anguish also causes them to reject their impotence, by attempting

> . . . to restore [their] capacity to act. But can [they], and how? One way is to submit to and identify with a person or group having power. By this symbolic participation in another person's life, [men have] the illusion of acting, when in reality [they] only submit to and become a part of those who act.[5]

*　　　　*　　　　*

Those truly committed to liberation must reject the banking concept in its entirety, adopting instead a concept of men as conscious beings, and consciousness as consciousness intent upon the world. They must abandon the educational goal of deposit-making and replace it with the posing of the problems of men in their relations with the world. "Problem-posing" education, responding to the essence of consciousness—*intentionality*—rejects communiqués and embodies communication. It epitomizes the special characteristic of consciousness: being *conscious of*, not only as intent on objects but as turned in upon itself in a Jasperian "split"—consciousness as consciousness *of* consciousness.

Liberating education consists in acts of cognition, not transferrals of information. It is a learning situation in which the cognizable object (far from being the end of the cognitive act) intermediates the cognitive actors—teacher on the one hand and students on the other. Accordingly, the practice of problem-posing education entails at the outset that the teacher-student contradiction be resolved. Dialogical relations—indispensable to the capacity of cognitive actors to cooperate in perceiving the same cognizable object—are otherwise impossible.

Indeed, problem-posing education, which breaks with the vertical patterns characteristic of banking education, can fulfill its function as the practice of freedom only if it can overcome the above contradiction. Through dialogue, the teacher-of-the-students and the students-of-the-teacher cease to exist and a new term emerges: teacher-student with students-teachers. The teacher is no longer merely the-one-who-teaches, but one who is himself taught in dialogue with the

4. *Ibid.,* p. 31.
5. *Ibid.*

students, who in turn while being taught also teach. They become jointly responsible for a process in which all grow. In this process, arguments based on "authority" are no longer valid; in order to function, authority must be *on the side of* freedom, not *against* it. Here, no one teaches another, nor is anyone self-taught. Men teach each other, mediated by the world, by the cognizable objects which in banking education are "owned" by the teacher.

The banking concept (with its tendency to dichotomize everything) distinguishes two stages in the action of the educator. During the first, he cognizes a cognizable object while he prepares his lessons in his study or his laboratory; during the second, he expounds to his students about that object. The students are not called upon to know, but to memorize the contents narrated by the teacher. Nor do the students practice any act of cognition, since the object towards which that act should be directed is the property of the teacher rather than a medium evoking the critical reflection of both teacher and students. Hence in the name of the "preservation of culture and knowledge" we have a system which achieves neither true knowledge nor true culture.

The problem-posing method does not dichotomize the activity of the teacher-student: he is not "cognitive" at one point and "narrative" at another. He is always "cognitive," whether preparing a project or engaging in dialogue with the students. He does not regard cognizable objects as his private property, but as the object of reflection by himself and the students. In this way, the problem-posing educator constantly re-forms his reflections in the reflection of the students. The students—no longer docile listeners—are now critical coinvestigators in dialogue with the teacher. The teacher presents the material to the students for their consideration, and reconsiders his earlier considerations as the students express their own. The role of the problem-posing educator is to create, together with the students, the conditions under which knowledge at the level of the *doxa* is superseded by true knowledge, at the level of the *logos*.

Whereas banking education anesthetizes and inhibits creative power, problem-posing education involves a constant unveiling of reality. The former attempts to maintain the *submersion* of consciousness; the latter strives for the *emergence* of consciousness and *critical intervention* in reality.

Students, as they are increasingly posed with problems relating to themselves in the world and with the world, will feel increasingly challenged and obliged to respond to that challenge. Because they apprehend the challenge as interrelated to other problems within a total context, not as a theoretical question, the resulting comprehension tends to be increasingly critical and thus constantly less alienated. Their response to the challenge evokes new challenges, followed by new understandings; and gradually the students come to regard themselves as committed.

Education as the practice of freedom—as opposed to education as the practice of domination—denies that man is abstract, isolated, independent, and unattached to the world; it also denies that the world exists as a reality apart from men. Authentic reflection considers neither abstract man nor the world without men, but men in their relations with the world. In these relations consciousness and world are simultaneous: consciousness neither precedes the world nor follows it. . . .

In problem-posing education, men develop their power to perceive critically *the way they exist* in the world *with which* and *in which* they find themselves; they come to see the world not as a static reality, but as a reality in process, in transformation. Although the dialectical relations of men with the world exist independently of how these relations are perceived (or whether or not they are perceived at all), it is also true that the form of action men adopt is to a large extent a function of how they perceive themselves in the world. Hence, the teacher-student and the students-teachers reflect simultaneously on themselves and the world without dichotomizing this reflection from action, and thus establish an authentic form of thought and action.

Once again, the two educational concepts and practices under analysis come into conflict. Banking education (for obvious reasons) attempts, by mythicizing reality, to conceal certain facts which explain the way men exist in the world; problem-posing education sets itself the task of demythologizing. Banking education resists dialogue; problem-posing education regards dialogue as indispensable to the act of cognition which unveils reality. Banking education treats students as objects of assistance; problem-posing education makes them critical thinkers. Banking education inhibits creativity and domesticates (although it cannot completely destroy) the *intentionality* of consciousness by isolating consciousness from the world, thereby denying men their ontological and historical vocation of becoming more fully human. Problem-posing education bases itself on creativity and stimulates true reflection and action upon reality, thereby responding to the vocation of men as beings who are authentic only when engaged in inquiry and creative transformation. In sum: banking theory and practice, as immobilizing and fixating forces, fail to acknowledge men as historical beings; problem-posing theory and practice take man's historicity as their starting point.

Problem-posing education affirms men as beings in the process of *becoming*—as unfinished, uncompleted beings in and with a likewise unfinished reality. Indeed, in contrast to other animals who are unfinished, but not historical, men know themselves to be unfinished;

they are aware of their incompletion. In this incompletion and this awareness lie the very roots of education as an exclusively human manifestation. The unfinished character of men and the transformational character of reality necessitate that education be an ongoing activity.

Education is thus constantly remade in the praxis. In order to *be*, it must *become*. Its "duration" (in the Bergsonian meaning of the word) is found in the interplay of the opposites *permanence* and *change*. The banking method emphasizes permanence and becomes reactionary; problem-posing education—which accepts neither a "well-behaved" present nor a predetermined future—roots itself in the dynamic present and becomes revolutionary.

Problem-posing education is revolutionary futurity. Hence it is prophetic (and, as such, hopeful). Hence, it corresponds to the historical nature of man. Hence, it affirms men as beings who transcend themselves, who move forward and look ahead, for whom immobility represents a fatal threat, for whom looking at the past must only be a means of understanding more clearly what and who they are so that they can more wisely build the future. Hence, it identifies with the movement which engages men as beings aware of their incompletion—an historical movement which has its point of departure, its subjects and its objective.

The point of departure of the movement lies in men themselves. But since men do not exist apart from the world, apart from reality, the movement must begin with the men-world relationship. Accordingly, the point of departure must always be with men in the "here and now," which constitutes the situation within which they are submerged, from which they emerge, and in which they intervene. Only by starting from this situation—which determines their perception of it—can they begin to move. To do this authentically they must perceive their state not as fated and unalterable, but merely as limiting—and therefore challenging.

Whereas the banking method directly or indirectly reinforces men's fatalistic perception of their situation, the problem-posing method presents this very situation to them as a problem. As the situation becomes the object of their cognition, the naïve or magical perception which produced their fatalism gives way to perception which is able to perceive itself even as it perceives reality, and can thus be critically objective about that reality.

A deepened consciousness of their situation leads men to apprehend that situation as an historical reality susceptible of transformation. Resignation gives way to the drive for transformation and inquiry, over which men feel themselves to be in control. If men, as historical beings necessarily engaged with other men in a movement of inquiry, did not control that movement, it would be (and is) a violation of men's humanity. Any situation in which some men prevent others from engaging in the process of inquiry is one of violence. The means used are not important; to alienate men from their own decision-making is to change them into objects.

This movement of inquiry must be directed towards humanization —man's historical vocation. The pursuit of full humanity, however, cannot be carried out in isolation or individualism, but only in fellowship and solidarity; therefore it cannot unfold in the antagonistic relations between oppressors and oppressed. No one can be authentically human while he prevents others from being so. Attempting *to be more* human, individualistically, leads to *having more*, egotistically: a form of dehumanization. Not that it is not fundamental *to have* in order *to be* human. Precisely because it *is* necessary, some men's *having* must not be allowed to constitute an obstacle to others' *having*, must not consolidate the power of the former to crush the latter.

Problem-posing education, as a humanist and liberating praxis, posits as fundamental that men subjected to domination must fight for their emancipation. To that end, it enables teachers and students to become subjects of the educational process by overcoming authoritarianism and an alienating intellectualism; it also enables men to overcome their false perception of reality. The world—no longer something to be described with deceptive words—becomes the object of that transforming action by men which results in their humanization.

Problem-posing education does not and cannot serve the interests of the oppressor. No oppressive order could permit the oppressed to begin to question: Why? While only a revolutionary society can carry out this education in systematic terms, the revolutionary leaders need not take full power before they can employ the method. In the revolutionary process, the leaders cannot utilize the banking method as an interim measure, justified on grounds of expediency, with the intention of *later* behaving in a genuinely revolutionary fashion. They must be revolutionary—that is to say, dialogical—from the outset.

The Education of Feeling

M. V. C. JEFFREYS

. . . There are two aspects of education at all levels which are worth special attention because they are both closely related to problems already referred to—the rediscovery of a coherent view of life, the conditions of effective communication, and the promotion of voluntary activity within the highly organized society. These two aspects of education are the education of feeling and the education of thinking.

There is as much need for the education of feeling as for the education of thinking. The one cannot be left to chance any more than the other. And, although the general emphasis in educational practice is by no means so preponderantly intellectual as it was fifty years ago, it is open to question whether we have yet appreciated all that the education of feeling involves. There is little doubt that the rather narrowly academic channel of the grammar school and the university still achieves intellectual distinction at the price of neglecting the education of feeling. . . .

It would be a great mistake to think of the education of feeling as a distinct area or department of education which can be promoted or neglected independently of the rest of the educational process. A human being is, or ought to be, a whole organism; and what affects one part affects the rest also. It is the business of education to foster the growth of balanced, whole persons. If education is deficient on the side of feeling, it is bound to be defective on the intellectual side; the resulting intellectual life will tend to be arid—it will, so to speak, lack body. Those who have studied the origins of music and drama in the primitive forms of dance know that the dance is a mainspring of human activity, a basic means of communication and inspiration. African tribal dances preparatory to a hunting expedition are not mere rituals; they are vital means of evoking and expressing the excitement and zest of the chase, with an elemental power far beyond anything that could be released by a deliberative assembly or even impassioned oratory.

"The Education of Feeling." From M. V. C. Jeffreys, *Personal Values in the Modern World* (London: Penguin Books, 1962), chapter 9, excerpted. Copyright © 1962, 1966 by M. V. C. Jeffreys. Reprinted by permission of the publisher.

Although there is no analogy between tribal dances and the folk-dancing that is practised in our modern society (for the latter has lost any concrete connexions it may once have had with practical social needs), it is nevertheless found that folk-dancing has a valuable contribution to make, not only to the physical and aesthetic education of boys and girls, but to their whole growth as people, including their capacity for sensitive and considerate social relations and also for lively intellectual response.

An essential part of our job as educators is to help people to achieve depth and sincerity of feeling. There is an emotional shallowness which, in those who have never been deeply stirred in their personal experience, often goes with intellectual shallowness; and is fostered by habitual exposure to the second-hand feeling of mass entertainment. But there is also an emotional shallowness of the intellectual who, through a fear of being swept off his precarious intellectual balance, fastidiously withdraws himself from the current of popular sentiment and the sources of group loyalty. He finds a sophisticated compromise by making light of occasions which stir public feelings (for example, a coronation); by adopting a patronizing attitude towards popular sentiment he can sterilize emotion. In this way some of the most highly educated and gifted individuals may be cut off from participating in the emotional life of the people, and thus unfitted to be leaders. For it is quite certain that no one can be a public leader who cannot enter into the feelings of the people at large. A leader should certainly be able to see beyond, and think beyond, the range of ordinary people. But, unless he can feel with ordinary people, he cannot interpret them to themselves or set before them a vision that they can understand. He must be able to talk their language; and language is rooted in feeling.

For the health and wholeness of personality it is as important that people should feel their own feelings as think their own thoughts. That is to say, wholeness of personality involves authenticity, integrity, and depth of feeling. Failure of genuine, deep feeling may be due to the fact that deep feeling has never been awakened in personal experience; the individual has been able to float along the surface of life. It may be due to emotional inhibition, especially by fear; the individual is for some reason unable to face life as it is and contrives to substitute counterfeit situations for real experience. Or it may be a loss of capacity resulting from the abuse of feeling; if the mere sensation of emotional situations is indulged in for its own sake, genuine feeling may become impossible. A girl who had flirted indiscriminately said: "I couldn't think of marriage until I can really feel deeply again."

For convenience of discussion, aesthetic and moral feeling may be distinguished. But this distinction must not be taken to imply any real separation, any more than there is any ultimate separation between feeling and thinking. We function as whole beings.

AESTHETIC FEELING

. . . To talk about experience is not the same thing as to undergo experience; in fact, talking about experience can be a way of keeping experience at arm's length. Our education is still inadequate from the point of view of creating opportunity for genuine experience. We all know the literature lessons which, especially under pressure of examinations, consist of biographical and critical notes by means of which the pupil can be forearmed against the examiner. He has the information for which he may be asked, and he knows what he ought to think about the literature prescribed for study. But what direct and genuine impact has the literature made upon the pupil, and what authentic response has he made to it? Undergoing experience is a different thing from memorizing facts; and we tend to forget that an opinion becomes a fact when it is someone else's opinion.

Some simple practical principles may be suggested for the education of aesthetic feeling:

1. *The principle of Do-it-yourself. Children should be given the opportunity to try their hands at a variety of arts and crafts—woodwork, pottery, dance, music, drama.* The purpose of this kind of experience is not necessarily to achieve a high degree of skill. The achievement of something like mastery of at least one art or craft is of great value in building up the personality. But there is another value in trying one's hand at a wide variety of skills. Practical experience, however limited and unsuccessful, gives an insight into what a particular art or craft involves which cannot be obtained in any other way. No amount of academic study of works of art, valuable as it may be, can take the place of practical experience. One may, for example, be an authority on pottery and one may have watched the deceptively easy operations of a skilled potter at his wheel and seen a pot apparently shape itself when charmed into existence by his fingers. But half-an-hour's inept struggles with a wheel and a lump of clay will teach one more of what the potter's craft means than years of observation and study. A day spent, under supervision, helping to excavate the site of a Roman villa will teach one more about the way in which an archaeologist goes about his work than all the books and photographs one can lay hands on. To try one's own hand at playing a musical instrument or at painting will give one a healthy respect for these arts which one will never get from listening and looking. It is part of education to watch a skill really well performed (be it painting, skating, or juggling); but it is also part of education—and a chastening part—to try one's own incompetent hand at it.

2. *Children should be given the opportunity to know the best that has been done in an art or craft—to see really good painting (in the*

original), hear good music really well played, or see a Shakespeare play really well staged and acted. Only so can they have good standards. There is a use for reproductions of paintings; but reproductions are misleading unless one knows how to make allowance for the difference between reproduction and original. Children, who will one day have to furnish their homes, should have a chance to see well-designed furniture and china, compare good design with bad, and realize that the most expensive things are not necessarily the best designed. The trouble with many people whose taste is bad is that they have never really encountered the best things, or encountered them well done. It is foolishly optimistic to expect that people will necessarily love the highest when they see it. But, if they do not see it, they cannot love it; while, if they see it, there is at least a sporting chance.

3. *The wise teacher does not get between the child and the experience. He lets the experience sink in.* He lets the music or the picture or the poem speak for itself. He knows the value of silence. There is a place and a time for critical analysis and discussion; and our enjoyment of any artistic experience is enhanced by an intelligent understanding of what we are enjoying and why we enjoy it. But before analysis of experience can be profitable there must be some experience to analyse. When music has been played or poetry spoken, it is inexpedient to fall upon it instantly with a dissecting knife or butcher's cleaver. The overanxious teacher's desire to interpret may result only in stifling the pupil's authentic response and substituting a manufactured response. Children themselves become so accustomed to giving the answers which they think the teacher expects that it may be hard work to convince them that their own sincere response is far more important than what the teacher thinks or what the book says. Some years ago a colleague of mine strove throughout the greater part of a poetry lesson with a junior class to get from the children what they really thought of the poem. At long last a child put up her hand and asked, in excited half-belief: "Oh! Miss, do you *want* what we *think?*" If children are to respond honestly to experience, experience must not be immediately pulled to pieces by the teacher, as one might catch a butterfly and pull its wings off. After many years I still remember the simple but impressive spectacle of a group of children, aged perhaps seven or eight, . . . who listened to a piece of music on a gramophone. When the music stopped the children, like Sherlock Holmes's dog in the night, did nothing. They remained seated quietly on the floor, for a few moments of silence, that rare commodity in the traffic of education.

In discussing the education of feeling and of thinking it should be emphasized that there can be no question of dividing the curriculum into subjects that have to be "felt" and others that have to be "thought." The business of redressing the balance of the curriculum is not simply a matter of putting more art, music, and "movement" into the timetable. In all learning there is room for feeling and for thinking. The enjoyment of art is greater if it is intelligently critical. And there is room for emotion in science and mathematics; beauty and wonder properly belong to scientific inquiry. Not only is wonder a spur to thought; it is also a governor of thought, promoting a spirit of reverence rather than of exploitation. Thought and feeling nourish one another.

MORAL FEELING

The health and growth of personality require that the person should be responsible for his behaviour. Conduct which is merely conditioned by the social environment has no more moral significance than a reflex movement. If we consider what should be the basic motive of responsible moral behaviour, we have to remind ourselves that the ground of all morality is respect of person for person. It is an important part of moral education to help those who are being educated to see how moral codes are rooted in respect for personality and do not consist merely of arbitrary rules. The breakdown of traditional moral authorities makes it all the more important in education to help young people to grasp the principles that underlie codes of conduct. Only by doing so can they learn to distinguish between those rules of conduct which can and should change with changing circumstances (that is, which are relative), and those principles which, if true at all, are true always and everywhere. If a caveman drags off his neighbour's wife by the hair, the outraged husband is morally entitled to pick up his club and take what measures may be necessary to correct his rival's behaviour. A different code is required in a highly organized society with an efficient legal system. But in both cases the ultimate purpose of the action taken is to obtain justice—to secure a state of affairs in which a proper respect of person for person is safeguarded. Again, in the kind of society to which most of us are accustomed, the practice of monogamy is held to maintain personal values at the highest level. My wife would consider that I was treating her with less than proper respect and esteem if I were to take several others at the same time; even if I assured her that she would have the status of chief wife, she would still feel insulted. In another kind of society, however, where eligible women cannot move about freely and safely without protection, monogamy may not be the best way of maintaining personal values, and polygamy may in fact preserve these values better.

Failure to distinguish between underlying, abiding principles and the changing expressions of those principles is a mark of limited minds which, to escape the difficulty of thinking things out, ascribe absolute value to precepts or customs which have only a relative validity. The same attitude of mind, which does not distinguish between relative and changing codes and ultimate and abiding principles, is also liable to confuse morals and manners. Thus a schoolboy may not see much difference of kind between a failure to tell the truth and a failure to wear his cap at the right angle or to leave the right button of his jacket unbuttoned.

No doubt there are people whose natural limitations make them incapable of a rational morality, and who can never advance beyond a state in which they are conditioned to do certain things and not to do certain other things. However that may be, it is the business of education to develop as fully as possible whatever capacity people have for an intelligent approach to moral problems. Every individual must pass through the stages of prior morality—response to physical pleasure and pain and response to social praise and blame—before reaching the mature stage of doing or not doing things because he has thought the problems out and made up his mind that he ought to act in this way or that—and, having made up his mind, is willing to be held responsible for his choices. The educator's business is to help boys and girls to grow—gradually, and often unevenly—into this third and mature stage of morality.

Moral education cannot be done by precept merely. In the last resort it can be done only through experience of the right kind of community life—by living in a community which is educative because the prevailing values and relations are good. In a school or family, a heavy share of responsibility for upholding the right values rests upon the adult members. If a teacher is to educate personal integrity and respect for the personality of others, he must himself possess these things in sufficient measure. He must also have humility, recognizing that education is a relationship of persons in which both teacher and pupil learn and are changed. One of the first things for a teacher to get into his head is that, if he is not learning, he is not teaching.

The question is sometimes asked whether a teacher ought to indoctrinate or to leave the pupil free to make up his own mind. Put in this way the question confuses the issue and cannot be answered, for the antithesis which it implies is false. The truth is that the good teacher can (and indeed must) reveal his opinions on matters of moment, but also can and should cherish the pupil's freedom to do his own thinking about what is offered to him.

Ralph Harper, in *Modern Philosophies and Education,* writes: "A passionless teacher is a bad teacher. But there are passions that are better left out of the classroom, especially the passion to display one's self. Another is a passion for a system or an idea or point of view that discourages reflection. Two normal passions remain: (a) a passion for the truth of any question that arises or ought to arise in the development of a subject-matter, the truth no matter how strictly one is forced to review one's previous judgments; and (b) a passion for the end of teaching, the autonomous functioning of the pupil's mind and habitual exercise by him of a character that is free, charitable, and self-moving." That is to say, there are two passions which must not be allowed to frustrate or neutralize one another: a passion for truth, at whatever cost to one's previous opinions; and a passion for the proper autonomy and freedom of the pupil's mind. It is far more important that the pupil should do his own thinking (provided he is sincerely seeking the truth) than that he should think the "right" things (the "right" things being the things the teacher would like him to think).

The teacher should not try to be neutral. In any case an attempt to appear neutral is unlikely to be successful. But, apart from the impossibility of concealing opinions, the teacher has an obligation to give his pupils the security which comes from being with people of firm beliefs and opinions, who know their own minds. A boy may reject his father's or his teacher's religious or political opinions; but he will have gained something from associating with someone whose character is rooted in firm belief which could never be gained from a person of uncertain mind.

The teacher, then, ought to be a real person with positive attitudes, not a mere transmitting medium. He should put his cards on the table and at the same time give his pupils the means of evaluating the different points of view that he will encounter. The pupil cannot make up his own mind if his mind remains empty; he must be fed with knowledge and exercised by meeting points of view. The teacher must be patient with his pupils' groping and tolerant of their brashness. But there is an important distinction between the tolerance that springs from charity and the tolerance that is only another name for indifference. It is the teacher's business to combat everything that disintegrates human personality, undermines the value set upon persons as such, or reduces human life to subhuman terms. He must vigilantly reckon with all those influences in modern life which numb the sense of responsibility, invite escape from responsibility, including those interpretations of human behaviour which sanction, or appear to sanction, the view that we cannot help being what we are.

Moral education is not easy in a world of shifting and confused values. The traditional, prudential basis of morality is an insecure educational foundation in an age when the traditional virtues are no longer supported by obvious expediency. It is unfortunate that moral education ever was based on prudential considerations; for, now that the prudential foundations of morality have to a large extent collapsed, or appear to have collapsed, we are left wondering what we can base our moral education upon.

If we do not appeal to prudential motives, we must appeal to the motives which in fact inspire all the best and most admirable human enterprise—the spirit of adventure, the idealism which puts the cause before personal safety and convenience, the sense of dedication in which self is swallowed up in something more than self. Kenneth Grahame spoke of "the demand of youth for long odds." Much delinquency is due to the best qualities gone wrong. Often the adolescent's urge to see himself in an admired character needs only a touch one way or the other to tip the scales of his admiration from criminal to saint.

The late Dr. McAllister Brew said that young people need three things above all:

1. Freedom to experiment and adventure. They need challenging experiences such as Outward Bound courses offer.

2. Security to depend upon—especially the security of dependable personal relations.

3. A faith—something to believe in which can take them out of themselves.

There are certain practical things that we can do—or try to do—to help young people in their moral development.

1. We can set before them the inspiring examples of people who, in all kinds of ways, found something more worthwhile than their own comfort and safety—who lost themselves to find their true selves. Example is worth a great deal more than precept, and biography offers an almost unlimited range of example. The great adventures of the human spirit are the heritage of our children, and they have a right to enter into it. We can show them explorers, like Nansen or Edward Wilson; scientists, like Faraday or the Curies; fighters, like Douglas Bader or Richard Hilary; workers to relieve human suffering, like Florence Nightingale, Kagawa, or Gladys Aylward. In presenting the lives of heroic characters, we should avoid the mistake of idealizing them. Their common humanity with ourselves is important. What they have done we might be able to do. The schoolteachers of Norway, who made such a magnificent stand against the Quisling government during the German occupation—a resistance in which they were splendidly supported by their pupils—were ordinary people like ourselves, raised to a higher power by the challenge of events.

2. We can set before our pupils the obligation to make one's own choice, and not take refuge behind public opinion or prevailing fashion. It is not easy for the young to take their own line in matters of principle, and to do what they honestly believe to be right because it is right, not to do what other people do because other people do it. What other people do may be right; and the young have to learn not to be rebels for the sake of rebelling as well as not to conform for the sake of conforming. But if what others do is right, it is not right *because* they do it. Boys and girls need a great deal of help, given with sympathetic understanding, in learning to stand on their own feet. Their contemporaries are neither understanding nor tolerant, and can be more exacting and tyrannical than any grown-ups. When one is fifty, one's contemporaries are blandly tolerant of one's nonconformities. When one is fifteen one may have to face persecution for trifling deviations.

The great lesson of the Existentialists is their insistence on inescapable personal responsibility. Even the pessimistic, atheistic writers refuse to take refuge in the illusion that we cannot help being what we are. Sartre, looking despair in the face, says: "We do not do what we want, and yet we are responsible for what we are." If the cynicism of this spirit makes some appeal to contemporary youth, so also should its courage.

3. Most important of all, we should do all we can to give young people opportunity to experience, in the right kind of social group, the meaning of fellowship. What kind of community the school is matters far more than what kind of instruction is given there. The school ought to offer both the security of a group loyalty which transcends individual likes and dislikes, and also the challenge of situations that demand some courage and resource. It should offer a prevailing atmosphere of wholesome values, especially the proper appreciation of those things which money cannot buy, such as friendship, good conversation, and the satisfaction of achievement.

The school in these days is no self-contained community. The revolution in school architecture during the last half-century symbolizes a change of outlook. We no longer surround our schools with high walls and locked gates to prevent those within from getting out and those without from getting in. And we no longer set the windows so high that no one can look in or out. The modern school building, often graciously surrounded by gardens, is open to the world and suggests that education is one of the social activities in which the neighbourhood is engaged. Parents are welcome and are encouraged to discuss their problems. The school plays its part in promoting good family relations. Through the youth employment service the school helps to pass on its boys and girls into adult life. Many schools, although administered by local authorities, are in active relation with neighbouring churches. In one way or another the school, as we now think of it in this country, is an educative community in which young people can grow as persons; but not an insulated community. The school rather is a community where social relations of many kinds have their origin. The danger in these days is not that the school will be merely a place of academic instruction, but rather that its social connexions will proliferate, and its general responsibilities multiply, to such an extent that no body of teachers can be expected to cope with all that has to be done.

The Freedom to Learn

CARL R. ROGERS

I wish to begin this [essay] with a statement which may seem surprising to some and perhaps offensive to others. It is simply this: Teaching, in my estimation, is a vastly overrated function.

Having made such a statement, I scurry to the dictionary to see if I really mean what I say. Teaching means "to instruct." Personally I am not much interested in instructing another in what he should know or think. "To impart knowledge or skill." My reaction is, why not be more efficient, using a book or programmed learning? "To make to know." Here my hackles rise. I have no wish to *make* anyone know something. "To show, guide, direct." As I see it, too many people have been shown, guided, directed. So I come to the conclusion that I *do* mean what I said. Teaching is, for me, a relatively unimportant and vastly overvalued activity.

But there is more in my attitude than this. I have a negative reaction to teaching. Why? I think it is because it raises all the wrong questions. As soon as we focus on teaching the question arises, what shall we teach? What, from our superior vantage point, does the other person need to know? I wonder if, in this modern world, we are justified in the presumption that we are wise about the future and the young are foolish. Are we *really* sure as to what they should know? Then there is the ridiculous question of coverage. What shall the course cover? This notion of coverage is based on the assumption that what is taught is what is learned; what is presented is what is assimilated. I know of no assumption so obviously untrue. One does not need research to provide evidence that this is false. One needs only to talk with a few students.

But I ask myself, "Am I so prejudiced against teaching that I find no situation in which it is worthwhile?" I immediately think of my experiences in Australia, not so long ago. I became much interested in the Australian aborigine. Here is a group which for more than 20,000 years has managed to live and exist in a desolate environment in which modern man would perish within a few days. The secret of the aborigine's survival has been teaching. He has passed on to the young every shred of knowledge about how to find water, about how to track game, about how to kill the kangaroo, about how to find his way through the trackless desert. Such knowledge is conveyed to the young as being *the* way to behave, and any innovation is frowned upon. It is clear that teaching has provided him the way to survive in a hostile and relatively unchanging environment.

Now I am closer to the nub of the question which excites me. Teaching and the imparting of knowledge make sense in an unchanging environment. This is why it has been an unquestioned function for centuries. But if there is one truth about modern man, it is that he lives in an environment which is *continually changing*. The one thing I can be sure of is that the physics which is taught to the present-day student will be outdated in a decade. The teaching in psychology will certainly be out of date in twenty years. The so-called "facts of history" depend very largely upon the current mood and temper of the culture. Chemistry, biology, genetics, sociology, are in such flux that a firm statement made today will almost certainly be modified by the time the student gets around to using the knowledge.

We are, in my view, faced with an entirely new situation in education where the goal of education, if we are to survive, is the *facilitation of change and learning*. The only man who is educated is the man who has learned how to learn; the man who has learned how to adapt and change; the man who has realized that no knowledge is secure, that only the process of *seeking* knowledge gives a basis for security. Changingness, a reliance on *process* rather than upon static knowledge, is the only thing that makes any sense as a goal for education in the modern world.

So now with some relief I turn to an activity, a purpose, which really warms me—the facilitation of learning. When I have been able to transform a group—and here I mean all the members of a group, myself included—into a community of *learners*, then the excitement has been almost beyond belief. To free curiosity; to permit individuals to go charging off in new directions dictated by their own interests; to unleash the sense of inquiry; to open everything to questioning and exploration; to recognize that everything is in process of change—here is an experience I can never forget. I cannot always achieve it in groups with which I am associated but when it is partially or largely achieved then it becomes a never-to-be-forgotten group experience. Out of such a context arise true students, real learners, creative scientists and scholars and practitioners, the kind of individuals who can live in a delicate but ever-changing balance between what is presently known and the flowing, moving, altering, problems and facts of the future.

Here then is a goal to which I can give myself wholeheartedly. I see *the facilitation of learning* as the *aim* of education, the way in which we might develop the learning man, the way in which we can learn to live as individuals in process. I see the facilitation of learning as the function which may hold constructive, tentative, changing, *process* answers to some of the deepest perplexities which beset man today.

But do we know how to achieve this new goal in education, or is it a will-o'-the-wisp which sometimes occurs, sometimes fails to occur, and thus offers little real hope? My answer is that we possess a very considerable knowledge of the conditions which encourage self-initiated, significant, experiential, "gut-level" learning by the whole person. We do not frequently see these conditions put into effect because they mean a real revolution in our approach to education and revolutions are not for the timid. But we do, as we have seen in the preceding chapters, find examples of this revolution in action.

We know—and I will briefly describe some of the evidence—that the initiation of such learning rests not upon the teaching skills of the leader, not upon his scholarly knowledge of the field, not upon his curricular planning, not upon his use of audiovisual aids, not upon the programmed learning he utilizes, not upon his lectures and presentations, not upon an abundance of books, though each of these might at one time or another be utilized as an important resource. No, the facilitation of significant learning rests upon certain attitudinal qualities which exist in the personal *relationship* between the facilitator and the learner.

TOO IDEALISTIC?

Some readers may feel that the belief that teachers can relate as persons to their students is hopelessly unrealistic and idealistic. They may see that in essence it is encouraging both teachers and students to be creative in their relationship to each other and in their relationship to subject matter, and feel that such a goal is quite impossible. They are not alone in this. I have heard scientists at leading schools of science and scholars in leading universities, arguing that it is absurd to try to encourage all students to be creative—we need hosts of mediocre technicians and workers and if a few creative scientists and artists and leaders emerge, that will be enough. That may be enough

for them. It may be enough to suit you. I want to go on record as saying it is *not* enough to suit me.

Let me try to state, somewhat more calmly and soberly, what I have
said with such feeling and passion.

I have said that it is most unfortunate that educators and the public
think about, and focus on, *teaching*. It leads them into a host of questions which are either irrelevant or absurd so far as real education is
concerned.

I have said that if we focused on the facilitation of *learning*—how,
why, and when the student learns, and how learning seems and feels
from the inside—we might be on a much more profitable track.

I have said that we have some knowledge, and could gain more,
about the conditions which facilitate learning, and that one of the
most important of these conditions is the attitudinal quality of the
interpersonal relationship between facilitator and learner. . . .

Those attitudes which appear effective in promoting learning can
be described. First of all is a transparent realness in the facilitator, a
willingness to be a person, to be and live the feelings and thoughts
of the moment. When this realness includes a prizing, a caring, a trust
and respect for the learner, the climate for learning is enhanced. When
it includes a sensitive and accurate empathic listening, then indeed a
freeing climate, stimulative of self-initiated learning and growth, exists.
The student is *trusted* to develop.

I have tried to make plain that individuals who hold such attitudes,
and are bold enough to act on them, do not simply modify classroom
methods—they revolutionize them. They perform almost none of the
functions of teachers. It is no longer accurate to call them teachers.
They are catalyzers, facilitators, giving freedom and life and the opportunity to learn, to students.

I have brought in the cumulating research evidence which suggests
that individuals who hold such attitudes are regarded as effective in
the classroom; that the problems which concern them have to do with
the release of potential, not the deficiencies of their students; that they
seem to create classroom situations in which there are not admired
children and disliked children, but in which affection and liking are
a part of the life of every child; that in classrooms approaching such
a psychological climate, children learn more of the conventional subjects.

But I have intentionally gone beyond the empirical findings to try
to take you into the inner life of the student—elementary, college, and
graduate—who is fortunate enough to live and learn in such an interpersonal relationship with a facilitator, in order to let you see what
learning feels like when it is free, self-initiated and spontaneous. I
have tried to indicate how it even changes the student-student relation-

ship—making it more aware, more caring, more sensitive, as well as increasing the self-related learning of significant material. I have spoken of the change it brings about in the faculty member.

Throughout, I have tried to indicate that if we are to have citizens who can live constructively in this kaleidoscopically changing world, we can *only* have them if we are willing for them to become self-starting, self-initiating learners. Finally, it has been my purpose to show that this kind of learner develops best, so far as we now know, in a growth-promoting, facilitative, relationship with a *person*.

The Will to Learn

JEROME S. BRUNER

The single most characteristic thing about human beings is that they learn. Learning is so deeply ingrained in man that it is almost involuntary, and thoughtful students of human behavior have even speculated that our specialization as a species is a specialization for learning. For, by comparison with organisms lower in the animal kingdom, we are ill equipped with prepared reflex mechanisms. As William James put it decades ago, even our instinctive behavior occurs only once, thereafter being modified by experience. With a half century's perspective on the discoveries of Pavlov, we know that man not only is conditioned by his environment, but may be so conditioned even against his will.

Why then invoke the idea of a "will to learn"? The answer derives from the idea of education, a human invention that takes a learner beyond "mere" learning. Other species begin their learning afresh each generation, but man is born into a culture that has as one of its principal functions the conservation and transmission of past learning. Given man's physical characteristics, indeed, it would be not only wasteful but probably fatal for him to reinvent even the limited range of technique and knowledge required for such a species to survive in the temperate zone. This means that man cannot depend upon a casual process of learning; he must be "educated." The young human must regulate his learning and his attention by reference to external requirements. He must eschew what is vividly right under his nose for what is dimly in a future that is often incomprehensible to him. And he must do so in a strange setting where words and diagrams and other abstractions suddenly become very important. School demands an orderliness and neatness beyond what the child has known before; it requires restraint and immobility never asked of him before; and often it puts him in a spot where he does not *know* whether he knows and can get no indication from anybody for minutes at a time as to whether he is on the right track. Perhaps most important of all, school is away from home with all that fact implies in anxiety, or challenge, or relief.

In consequence of all this the problem of "the will to learn" becomes important, indeed exaggerated. Let us not delude ourselves: it is a problem that cannot be avoided, though it can be made manageable, I think. We shall explore what kinds of factors lead to satisfaction in "educated" learning, to pleasure in the practice of learning as it exists in the necessarily artificial atmosphere of the school. Almost all children possess what have come to be called "intrinsic" motives for learning. An intrinsic motive is one that does not depend upon reward that lies outside the activity it impels. Reward inheres in the successful termination of that activity or even in the activity itself.

Curiosity is almost a prototype of the intrinsic motive. Our attention is attracted to something that is unclear, unfinished, or uncertain. We sustain our attention until the matter in hand becomes clear, finished, or certain. The achievement of clarity or merely the search for it is what satisfies. We would think it preposterous if somebody thought to reward us with praise or profit for having satisfied our curiosity. However pleasant such external reward might be, and however much we might come to depend upon it, the external reward is something added. What activates and satisfies curiosity is something inherent in the cycle of activity by which we express curiosity. Surely such activity is biologically relevant, for curiosity is essential to the survival not only of the individual but of the species. There is considerable research that indicates the extent to which even nonhuman primates will put forth effort for a chance to encounter something novel on which to exercise curiosity. But it is clear that unbridled curiosity is little more than unlimited distractibility. To be interested in everything that comes along is to be interested in nothing for long. Studies of the behavior of three-year-olds, for example, indicate the degree to which they are dominated from the outside by the parade of vivid impressions that pass their way. They turn to this bright color, that sharp sound, that new shiny surface. Many ends are beyond their reach, for they cannot sustain a steady course when the winds shift. If anything, they are "too curious." They live by what psychologists have long called the laws of primary attention: attention dominated by vividness and change in the environment. There has been much speculation about the function of this early and exhausting tempo of curiosity. One neuropsychologist, Donald Hebb, has suggested that the child is drinking in the world, better to construct his neural "models" of the environment. And it is plain that a stunted organism is produced by depriving an infant of the rich diet of impressions on which his curiosity normally feeds with such extravagance. Animals raised in homogenized environments show crippling deficits in their later ability to learn and to transfer what they have learned. Children "kept in the attic" by misguided or psychotic parents show the same striking backwardness. Indeed, even the children who have suffered the dull, aseptic environment of backward foundling homes often show a decline in intelligence that can be compensated only by vigorous measures of enrichment. So surely, then, an important early function is served by the child's omnivorous capacity for new impressions. He is sorting the world, storing those things that have some recurrent regularity and require "knowing," discriminating them from the parade of random impressions.

But if attention is to be sustained, directed to some task and held there in spite of temptations that come along, then obviously constraints must be established. The voluntary deployment of curiosity, so slowly and painfully mastered, seems to be supported in part by the young child's new-found capacity to "instruct himself," literally to talk to himself through a sustained sequence. And in part the steadying force seems to be the momentum of concrete overt acts that have a way of sustaining the attention required for their completion by shutting off irrelevant impressions. In time, and with the development of habitual activities, and of language, there emerges more self-directed attention, sometimes called derived primary attention. The child is held steady not so much by vividness as by the habitual round of activity that now demands his attention. Little enough is known about how to help a child become master of his own attention, to sustain it over a long, connected sequence. But while young children are notoriously wandering in their attention, they can be kept in a state of rapt and prolonged attentiveness by being told compelling stories. There may be something to be learned from this observation. What makes the internal sequence of a story even more compelling than the distractions that lie outside it? Are there comparable properties inherent in other activities? Can these be used to train a child to sustain his curiosity beyond the moment's vividness?

Observe a child or group of children building a pile of blocks as high as they can get them. Their attention will be sustained to the flashing point until they reach the climax when the pile comes crashing down. They will return to build still higher. The drama of the task is only its minor virtue. More important is the energizing lure of uncertainty made personal by one's own effort to control it. It is almost the antithesis of the passive attraction of shininess and the vivid. To channel curiosity into more powerful intellectual pursuits requires precisely that there be this transition from the passive, receptive, episodic form of curiosity to the sustained and active form. There are games not only with objects, but with ideas and questions —like Twenty Questions—that provide such a disciplining of the channeling of curiosity. Insofar as one may count on this important human motive—and it seems among the most reliable of the motives —then it seems obvious that our artificial education can in fact be made less artificial from a motivational standpoint by relating it initially to the more surfacy forms of curiosity and attention, and then cultivating curiosity to more subtle and active expression. I think it is fair to say that most of the success in contemporary curriculum building has been achieved by this route. When success comes, it takes the form of recognition that beyond the few things we know there lies a domain of inference: that putting together the two and two that we have yields astonishing results. But this raises the issue of competence, to which we must turn next.

For curiosity is only one of the intrinsic motives for learning. The drive to achieve competence is another. Professor Robert White puts the issue well:

> According to Webster, competence means fitness or ability, and the suggested synonyms include capability, capacity, efficiency, proficiency, and skill. It is therefore a suitable word to describe such things as grasping and exploring, crawling and walking, attention and perception, all of which promote an effective—a competent—interaction with the environment. It is true, of course, that maturation plays a part in all these developments, but this part is heavily overshadowed by learning in all the more complex accomplishments like speech or skilled manipulation. I shall argue that it is necessary to make competence a motivational concept; there is *competence motivation* as well as competence in its more familiar sense of achieved capacity. The behavior that leads to the building up of effective grasping, handling, and letting go of objects, to take one example, is not random behavior that is produced by an overflow of energy. It is directed, selective, and persistent, and it continues not because it serves primary drives, which indeed it cannot serve until it is almost perfect, but because it satisfies an intrinsic need to deal with the environment.[1]

Observations of young children and of the young of other species suggest that a good deal of their play must be understood as practice in coping with the environment. Primatologists describe, for example, how young female baboons cradle infant baboons in their arms long before they produce their own offspring. In fact, baboon play can be seen almost entirely as the practice of interpersonal skills. Unlike human children, baboons never play with objects, and this, the anthropologists believe, is connected with their inability to use tools when they grow up. And there is evidence that early language mastery, too, depends on such early preparation. One linguist recently has shown how a two-year-old goes on exploring the limits of language use even

1. R. W. White, "Motivation Reconsidered: The Concept of Competence," *Psychological Review*, 66:297–333 (1959).

after the lights are out, parents removed, communication stopped, and sleep imminent.

The child's metalinguistic play is hard to interpret as anything other than pleasure in practicing and developing a new skill. Although competence may not "naturally" be directed toward school learning, it is certainly possible that the great access of energy that children experience when they "get into a subject they like" is made of the same stuff.

We get interested in what we get good at. In general, it is difficult to sustain interest in an activity unless one achieves some degree of competence. Athletics is the activity par excellence where the young need no prodding to gain pleasure from an increase in skill, save where prematurely adult standards are imposed on little leagues formed too soon to ape the big ones. A custom introduced some years ago at the Gordonstoun School in Scotland has become legendary. In addition to conventionally competitive track and field events within the school, there was established a novel competition in which boys pitted themselves against their own best prior record in the events. Several American schools have picked up the idea and, while there has been no "proper evaluation," it is said that the system creates great excitement and enormous effort on the part of the boys.

To achieve the sense of accomplishment requires a task that has some beginning and some terminus. Perhaps an experiment can serve again as a parable. There is a well-known phenomenon known to psychologists by the forbidding name of the Zeigarnik Effect. In brief, tasks that are interrupted are much more likely to be returned to and completed, and much more likely to be remembered, than comparable tasks that one has completed without interruption. But that puts the matter superficially, for it leaves out of account one factor that is crucial. The effect holds only if the tasks that the subject has been set are ones that have a structure—a beginning, a plan, and a terminus. If the tasks are "silly" in the sense of being meaningless, arbitrary, and without visible means for checking progress, the drive to completion is not stimulated by interruption.

It seems likely that the desire to achieve competence follows the same rule. Unless there is some meaningful unity in what we are doing and some way of telling how we are doing, we are not very likely to strive to excel ourselves. Yet surely this too is only a small part of the story, for everybody does not want to be competent in the same activities, and some competencies might even be a source of embarrassment to their possessors. Boys do not thrill to the challenge of sewing a fine seam (again, in our culture), nor girls to becoming competent street fighters. There are competencies that are appropriate and activating for different ages, the two sexes, different social classes. But there are some things about competence motives that transcend these particulars. One is that an activity (given that it is "approved"), must have some meaningful structure to it if it requires skill that is a little bit beyond that now possessed by the person—that it be learned by the exercise of effort. It is probably the combination of the two that is critical.

Experienced teachers who work with the newer curricula in science and mathematics report that they are surprised at the eagerness of students to push ahead to next steps in the course. Several of the teachers have suggested that the eagerness comes from increased confidence in one's ability to understand the material. Some of the students were having their first experience of understanding a topic in some depth, of going somewhere in a subject. It is this that is at the heart of competence motives, and surely our schools have not begun to tap this enormous reservoir of zest.

While we do not know the limits within which competence drives can be shaped and channeled by external reward, it seems quite likely that they are strongly open to external influence. But channelization aside, how can education keep alive and nourish a drive to competence —whether expressed in farming, football, or mathematics? What sustains a sense of pleasure and achievement in mastering things for their own sake—what Thorstein Veblen referred to as an instinct for workmanship? Do competence motives strengthen mainly on their exercise, in whatever context they may be exercised, or do they depend also upon being linked to drives for status, wealth, security, or fame?

There are, to begin with, striking differences among cultures and between strata within any particular society with respect to the encouragement given to competence drives. David McClelland, for example, in writing about the "achieving society," comments upon the fact that in certain times and places one finds a flowering of achievement motivation strongly supported by the society and its institutions and myths alike. Emphasis upon individual responsibility and initiative, upon independence in decision and action, upon perfectibility of the self—all of these things serve to perpetuate more basic competency motives past childhood.

But cultures vary in their evaluation of *intellectual* mastery as a vehicle for the expression of competence. Freed Bales, for example, in comparing Irish and Jewish immigrant groups in Boston, remarks that the Jewish, much more than the Irish, treat school success and intellectuality as virtues in their own right as well as ways of upward mobility. The reasons can be found in history. Herzog and Zborowski, in their book on eastern European Jewish communities, suggest that the barrier erected against Jews' entering other professions may have helped foster the cultivation of intellectual excellence as a prized expression of competence.

A culture does not "manage" these matters consciously by the applications of rewards and reproofs alone. The son of the rabbi in the eastern European *stetl* was not punished if he wished to become a merchant rather than a Talmudic scholar, and, indeed, if he chose to become the latter he typically went through long, extrinsically unrewarding, and arduous training to do so. More subtle forces are at work, all of them fairly familiar but too often overlooked in discussing education. One of them is "approval." The professional man is more "respected" than the manual worker. But that scarcely exhausts the matter. Respected by whom? Contemporary sociologists speak of the approval of one's "reference group"—those to whom one looks for guides to action, for the definition of the possible, for ultimate approbation. But what leads *this* individual to look to *that* particular reference group?

What appears to be operative is a process we cavalierly call identification. The fact of identification is more easily described than explained. It refers to the strong human tendency to model one's "self" and one's aspirations upon some other person. When we feel we have succeeded in "being like" an identification figure, we derive pleasure from the achievement and, conversely, we suffer when we have "let him down." Insofar as the identification figure is also "a certain kind of person"—belongs to some group or category—we extend our loyalties from an individual to a reference group. In effect, then, identification relates one not only to individuals, but to one's society as well.

While this account is oversimplified, it serves to underline one important feature of identification as a process—its self-sustaining nature. For what it accomplishes is to pass over to the learner the control of punishment and reward. Insofar as we now carry our standards with us, we achieve a certain independence from the immediate rewards and punishments meted out by others.

It has been remarked by psychologists that identification figures are most often those who control the scarce psychological resources that we most desire—love, approval, sustenance. Let me skip this issue for a moment and return to it later.

The term identification is usually reserved for those strong attachments where there is a considerable amount of emotional investment. But there are "milder" forms of identification that are also important during the years of childhood and after. Perhaps we should call those who serve in these milder relationships "competence models." They are the "on the job" heroes, the reliable ones with whom we can interact in some way. Indeed, they control a rare resource, some desired competence, but what is important is that the resource is attainable by interaction. The "on the job" model is nowhere better illustrated than in the manner in which the child learns language from a parent. The tryout-correction-revision process continues until the child comes to learn the rules whereby sentences are generated and transformed appropriately. Finally he develops a set of productive habits that enable him to be his own sentence maker and his own corrector. He "learns the rules of the language." The parent is the model who, by interaction, teaches the skill of language.

In the process of teaching a skill the parent or teacher passes on much more. The teacher imparts attitudes toward a subject and, indeed, attitudes toward learning itself. What results may be quite inadvertent. Often, in our schools, for example, this first lesson is that learning has to do with remembering things when asked, with maintaining a certain undefined tidiness in what one does, with following a train of thought that comes from outside rather than from within and with honoring right answers. Observant anthropologists have suggested that the basic values of the early grades are a stylized version of the feminine role in the society, cautious rather than daring, governed by a ladylike politeness.

One recent study by Pauline Sears underlines the point. It suggests that girls in the early grades, who learn to control their fidgeting earlier and better than boys, are rewarded for excelling in their "feminine" values. The reward can be almost too successful, so that in later years it is difficult to move girls beyond the orderly virtues they learned in their first school encounters. The boys, more fidgety in the first grade, get no such reward and as a consequence may be freer in their approach to learning in later grades. Far more would have to be known about the other conditions present in the lives of these children to draw a firm conclusion from the findings, but it is nonetheless suggestive. There are surely many ways to expand the range of competence models available to children. One is the use of a challenging master teacher, particularly in the early grades. And there is film or closed-circuit television, opening up enormously the range of teachers to whom the student can be exposed. Filmed teaching has, to be sure, marked limits, for the student cannot interact with an image. But a kind of pseudo interaction can be attained by including in the television lesson a group of students who are being taught right on the screen, with whom the student can take common cause. Team teaching provides still another approach to the exemplification of a range of competences, particularly if one of the teachers is charged specially with the role of gadfly. None of the above is yet a tried practice, but pedagogy, like economics and engineering, often must try techniques to find not only whether they work, but how they may be made to work.

I would like to suggest that what the teacher must be, to be an effective competence model, is a day-to-day working model with whom to interact. It is not so much that the teacher provides a model to *imitate*. Rather, it is that the teacher can become a part of the student's internal dialogue—somebody whose respect he wants, someone whose standards he wishes to make his own. It is like becoming a speaker of a language one shares with somebody. The language of that interaction becomes a part of oneself, and the standards of style and clarity that one adopts for that interaction become a part of one's own standards.

Finally, a word about one last intrinsic motive that bears closely upon the will to learn. Perhaps it should be called reciprocity. For it involves a deep human need to respond to others and to operate jointly with them toward an objective. One of the important insights of modern zoology is the importance of this intraspecies reciprocity for the survival of individual members of the species. The psychologist Roger Barker has commented that the best way he has found to predict the behavior of the children whom he has been studying in great detail in the midst of their everyday activities is to know their situations. A child in a baseball game behaves baseball; in the drugstore the same child behaves drugstore. Situations have a demand value that appears to have very little to do with the motives that are operative. Surely it is not simply a "motive to conform"; this is too great an abstraction. The man who is regulating his pressure on the back of a car, along with three or four others, trying to "rock it out," is not so much conforming as "fitting his efforts into an enterprise." It is about as primitive an aspect of human behavior as we know.

Like the other activities we have been discussing, its exercise seems to be its sole reward. Probably it is the basis of human society, this response through reciprocity to other members of one's species. Where joint action is needed, where reciprocity is required for the group to attain an objective, then there seem to be processes that carry the individual along into learning, sweep him into a competence that is required in the setting of the group. We know precious little about this primitive motive to reciprocate, but what we do know is that it can furnish a driving force to learn as well. Human beings (and other species as well) fall into a pattern that is required by the goals and activities of the social group in which they find themselves. "Imitation" is not the word for it, since it is usually not plain in most cases what is to be imitated. A much more interesting way of looking at what is involved is provided by the phenomenon of a young child learning to use the pronouns "I" and "you" correctly. The parent says to the child, "You go to bed now." The child says, "No, you no go to bed." We are amused. "Not *me* but *you*," we say. In time, and after a surprisingly brief period of confusion, the child learns that "you" refers to himself when another uses it, and to another person when he uses it—and the reverse with "I." It is a prime example of reciprocal learning. It is by much the same process that children learn the beautifully complicated games they play (adult and child games alike), that they learn their role in the family and in school, and finally that they come to take their role in the greater society.

The corpus of learning, using the word now as synonymous with knowledge, is reciprocal. A culture in its very nature is a set of values, skills, and ways of life that no one member of the society masters. Knowledge in this sense is like a rope, each strand of which extends no more than a few inches along its length, all being intertwined to give a solidity to the whole. The conduct of our educational system has been curiously blind to this interdependent nature of knowledge. We have "teachers" and "pupils," "experts" and "laymen." But the community of learning is somehow overlooked.

What can most certainly be encouraged—and what is now being developed in the better high schools—is something approximating the give and take of a seminar in which discussion is the vehicle of instruction. This is reciprocity. But it requires recognition of one critically important matter: you cannot have both reciprocity and the demand that everybody learn the same thing or be "completely" well rounded in the same way all the time. If reciprocally operative groups are to give support to learning by stimulating each person to join his efforts to a group, then we shall need tolerance for the specialized roles that develop—the critic, the innovator, the second helper, the cautionary. For it is from the cultivation of these interlocking roles that the participants get the sense of operating reciprocally in a group. Never mind that this pupil for this term in this seminar has a rather specialized task to perform. It will change. Meanwhile, if he can see how he contributes to the effectiveness of the group's operations on history or geometry or whatnot, he is likely to be the more activated. And surely one of the roles that will emerge is that of auxiliary teacher—let it, encourage it. It can only help in relieving the tedium of a classroom with one expert up here and the rest down there.

At the risk of being repetitious, let me restate the argument. It is this. The will to learn is an intrinsic motive, one that finds both its source and its reward in its own exercise. The will to learn becomes a "problem" only under specialized circumstances like those of a school, where a curriculum is set, students confined, and a path fixed. The problem exists not so much in learning itself, but in the fact that what the school imposes often fails to enlist the natural energies that sustain spontaneous learning—curiosity, a desire for competence, aspiration to emulate a model, and a deep-sensed commitment to the web of social reciprocity. Our concern has been with how these energies may be cultivated in support of school learning. If we know little firmly, at least we are not without reasonable hypotheses about how to proceed. The practice of education does, at least, produce interesting hypotheses. After all, the Great Age of Discovery was made possible by men whose hypotheses were formed before they had developed a decent technique for measuring longitude.

You will have noted by now a considerable deemphasis of "extrinsic" rewards and punishments as factors in school learning. There has been in these pages a rather intentional neglect of the so-called Law of Effect, which holds that a reaction is more likely to be repeated if it has previously been followed by a "satisfying state of affairs." I am not unmindful of the notion of reinforcement. It is doubtful, only, that "satisfying states of affairs" are *reliably* to be found outside learning itself—in kind or harsh words from the teacher, in grades and gold stars, in the absurdly abstract assurance to the high school student that his lifetime earnings will be better by 80 percent if he graduates. External reinforcement may indeed get a particular act going and may even lead to its repetition, but it does not nourish, reliably, the long course of learning by which man slowly builds in his own way a serviceable model of what the world is and what it can be.

Dewey Reconsidered

GEORGE DENNISON

The crisis in public education, like the hastening dissolution of other of our social institutions, creates anxiety and doubt, and we respond as anxious people do: we try to impose order by force, imagining that if we can obliterate the symptoms, we will have cured the disease. We speak increasingly of control, as if we feared that everything would collapse into nothing if we let loose our (illusory) hold on things. And so I have been urging one simple truth: . . . that the educational function does not rest upon our ability to control, or our will to instruct, but upon our human nature and the nature of experience. I have been trying to describe their attributes as they appear in action, for—in kind—they are the bases of all teaching and all learning. Dewey calls them the *starting point* of education. If these deeper attributes of our lives are often obscured by anxiety, they also survive it. They are the source of talents far stronger than our gift for bureaucratic planning. I have been urging that we trust them, that we show some little faith in the life principles which have in fact structured all the well-structured elements of our existence, such principles as our inherent sociability, our inherent rationality, our inherent freedom of thought, our inherent curiosity, and our inherent (while vigor lasts) appetite for more. What this means concretely is that we must rescue the individuals from their present obscurity in the bureaucratic heap: the students, because they are what this activity is all about; the teachers, because they are the ones who must act. . . .

It might be well to contrast Dewey's thought, and the style of his thought, his habit of mind, with the prevailing style of our educationists, not only to observe the difference between a philosopher and an Expert, but to see how and why our educational establishment is hostile to Dewey's deepest meanings (as it is hostile to the related philosophies of Neill and Tolstoy). And I must confess that I am not capable of performing this analysis impartially. Nor would there be

"Dewey Reconsidered." From George Dennison, *The Lives of Children* (New York: Random House, Inc., 1969), pp. 246–60, excerpted. Copyright © 1969 by George Dennison. Reprinted by permission of the publisher.

much point in performing it at all if it were not for the fact that organized mediocrity wields such power in our country at present. Where the influence of a philosopher rests upon the authority of his thought, the influence of our educationists rests upon professional connections with the centralized power of the educational establishment. Their thought, taken simply as thought, is often so feeble as to provoke astonishment. This is frequently true of the most influential of them all, Jerome S. Bruner, director of the Center for Cognitive Studies at Harvard. Bruner's books are not without their virtues, but I shall leave it to others to praise them. I would like to concentrate for a moment, in an admittedly biased, unfair, and perhaps ill-tempered way, upon an analysis of the characteristic failure that renders Bruner's contribution, in my opinion, pernicious. Nor am I speaking only of Bruner. His failings are characteristic of the field. The positive purpose of this negative critique will be evident in a moment.

Bruner's most recent book is *Toward a Theory of Instruction.* Its thought—compared to the actual practice of the public schools—seems to be enlightened and humane. It calls attention to inborn motives, natural curiosity, the give-and-take of all social affairs. It is based at every turn upon years of research. Yet there is a flaw in the grain. As such it is no great matter. But when it is transformed into the hard facts of the environment of the schools, it becomes—as I shall show—an important matter indeed.

Bruner describes the inborn motives of the will to learn, numbering among them "the deep-sensed commitment to the web of social reciprocity." . . .

Bruner's criteria here are not drawn from life, nature, experience, but from the closed system of the schools. He has addressed himself to the question, How can we improve our schools? Perhaps it is obvious that his answers are administrator's answers. It may not be obvious, however, that his question is the question of the technocrat. For given the current crisis in education, the question, How can we improve our schools? would satisfy neither the scientist nor the philosopher. Both would ask instead, How can we educate our young?

I would like to anatomize these thoughts of Bruner's. And I would like to do it in such a way as to make clear their ultimate environmental effect upon the young. If there is any doubt that the identical voice percolates endlessly downward through the pyramid of control, here are two other examples:

> What we would propose . . . is that we should learn still more about how children learn, and how different children learn differently, before any solutions are proposed. When we have enough data, we think it may be possible to construct a better fit between the objectives of the curriculum and the pupils' perceptions; and certainly a better fit be-

tween those objectives, the evaluative system, and the pupils' evaluative map.[1]

(These words are such a quintessence of the self-absorption of bureaucratic research, that I feel obliged to underline them, as it were, in red. Who would suppose that this educator was writing in 1968? Drop-outs, illiteracy, vandalism, savagery, loss of intelligence, loss of spirit, apathy rising into nausea, nausea rising into rage—these are the facts for many millions of pupils and families in their experience of the public schools. They are such facts as indicate the basic responsibility of educators. Yet how responsible this one manages to sound while she holds them at arm's length in deference to her trivial data, her "better fits" and "evaluative maps," and her animistic belief that the curriculum itself possesses "objectives"!)

There is no point in giving the other example.

And I would prefer not returning to Bruner, were it not for the fact that our society, in empowering its technocrats, has disenfranchised the scattered millions who might otherwise cohere into rational communities—the only adequate base for the educational function. It is no news that we have become a heartless technocracy. It may need to be said, however, that we are far along toward becoming a mindless one as well. This is the distinction I would like finally to make, the distinction between true thought, true mind, and mere intellection, for if ever a nation stood in need of wisdom (as I believe we can find in the pages of Dewey), our nation does, and needs it now.

How is thought reduced to mere intellection? Ultimately, as I shall try to show, by a failure of love. More obviously by failure of imagination, sympathy, observation—failure of response. Nor is the absence of response a merely negative phenomenon. We do not find a gap where response should be. We find instead the attempt to control. This displacement corresponds exactly to the failure of thought that we refer to when we speak disdainfully of "abstractions"; for we do not mean that thought should use no abstractions, but that when abstractions are allowed to usurp the place that belongs to what can only be called the body of the world, they no longer appear as vital components of thought, but as *mere* abstractions.

Bruner tells us that every child experiences a "deep-sensed commitment to the web of social reciprocity." Now in a rough-and-ready way this seems to be a true statement about life. At the same time it is quite obvious that children do not experience webs and commitments, but rather experience other children, adults, games, objects, etc. Are we haggling about words? Far from it. We want to speak of motives, desires, needs. We want to know how experience transpires for the child himself, and for the adult himself. We want to know what the

1. Mary Alice White, *The Urban Review*, April, 1968.

quick of it is, the life of it. It is fatal to our investigation to fall into the error of believing that our own abstract descriptions—"commitment to the web, etc."—actually transpire as facts in the immediate experience of those we are observing. To allow this to happen is to lose sight of the object of study. It is to begin to tabulate one's own abstractions under the impression that one is speaking, still, of the organic unfolding of life. Whether we are aware of it or not, we have begun to limit and control the phenomena. Let us look at the consequences of this failure. It is chronic, and its consequences are pervasive.

We see, first, that the essential philosophic and scientific question passes by. How shall we educate the young? Bruner is not interested. He speaks, rather, of instruction, and is concerned to improve its efficiency within the existing framework of the schools.

Now that high-sounding phrase, "deep-sensed commitment to the web of social reciprocity," appears in its true colors as the "give and take of a seminar." "This," he tells us, "is reciprocity." Is it? Is it not rather the Administrator himself, the Social Engineer, the School Monk, leaning back in his chair with his hands behind his head, his necktie informally awry, uncorking the Horn of Plenty by chatting with his students instead of subjecting them, as he might, to the terrors of a test? Reciprocity, social reciprocity, the web of social reciprocity, deep-sensed commitment . . . and we end with the "give and take of a seminar"! One would have thought that reciprocity referred to the peerage of existence, to our own approaching death and the extending life of the world in the lives of the young. And to the student's uniqueness, and to our own. And to the fact that experience, as it emerges, is always some way new, and always evolves in situations—situations, moreover, in which we can only give *our* part, not the other person's part. The questions that belong to reciprocity are questions of volition and of needs, the needs of the individual and those of society: Shall we compel the student's presence? Shall we compel his attention? Shall we "evaluate" him without his consent and for purposes of our own which we keep hidden? Shall we predetermine the duration and content of our encounter? Shall we prescribe in advance the limits of our own response, as we do prescribe them when we know so blandly, so deeply that we mean to instruct?

I think it is clear that when Bruner talks of reciprocity, he is thinking really, perhaps unknown to himself, of control, social engineering, manipulation. For we now discover that it is not the present lives of the students, their present interests, enthusiasms, aversions, loyalties, ideals, passions, rivalries, etc., that must be allowed to animate them in the classroom; but rather certain "roles" are available—"the critic, the innovator, the second helper, the cautionary"—and the wise administrator will guide the students in their exploration of these roles so that they "get the sense of operating reciprocally in a group"; and

God knows, get no sense whatever of being alive in the quick of other lives, the quick of exciting thoughts, earnest resolves, strokes of invention, wit, and perhaps (can it be said?) an ardent love of learning! If an educationist can say of a youth, "He assumed a role," the youth will have experienced everything *but* a role. He will have been fired by some idea, some response of understanding or conviction. His real desires will have leaped toward some real object or person. In "operating reciprocally," people do not "get the sense" of it at all, but are actually *engaged* with each other, for real.

How odd, really, our educationists are! They discover the autonomy of indwelling motives and patterned growth—and then insist on manipulating these autonomous things. They affirm the value of instinctual life—and propose systems which make it count for nothing. They proclaim a reverence for facts, and immure themselves for years in experimental labs, from which they emerge in a haze of abstractions, agreeing chiefly on one thing: that more research is needed. And when this research brings them to the truisms known to every mother, and they might at least rest, they haven't the modesty to admit it and hold still. (What vast researches Bruner cites in order to establish that babies poke around and look at things—"curiosity is the prototype of the intrinsic motive"; that the three-year-old girl wishes she could chop up her food as well as her five-year-old brother—"desire for competence and aspiration to emulate a model"; and that nine-year-old boys are quick to run errands, to suggest expedients, and love to be praised for their real as opposed to unreal contributions—"deep-sensed commitment to the web of social reciprocity.")

The environmental effect of this kind of thinking, this mere intellection, this failure of mind, is quite clear. The school itself becomes manipulative. And the manipulation is hard to resist, for it seems to rest upon such enlightened deference to "inborn motives" and "autonomous functions," though it violates and invades those functions at every turn, pinching the energies of life, rounding them off, arranging them, producing in the end a feeble image of growth, where what is wanted is growth itself.

If I have been ill-tempered in my complaint, let me relieve the monotone by giving the other example, after all:

> Now, while rules of deference may be asymmetrical and a superordinate person may have rights to certain familiarities or invasions of the metaphorical boundary around the self that the subordinate cannot reciprocate, yet the superordinate still must respect the subordinate and not press too far. Thus, while it may be expected that teachers have the right to touch pupils, particularly in a friendly manner, it would not be expected that the same right be freely exercised by pupils.

This choice lyric is from a book called *Realities of the Urban Classroom* (G. Alexander Moore, Jr.). It was financed by government and foundation money (the title alone deserves a grant), and is perhaps an example of the "data" Miss White tells us we need so much more of "before any solutions are proposed."

How different philosophic thought is from the technocratic intellection of which I have just given examples!

Education, for Dewey, is a function of experience and a fact of life, not the activity of a closed system of schools. Nor do schools introduce something different in kind into the experience of the child, but work with processes and capacities already given, already considerably developed:

> The educator who receives the child . . . has to find ways for doing consciously and deliberately what "nature" accomplishes in the earlier years.

It follows, then, that we must not set up conditions which violate the very processes upon which the enterprise rests. As I have mentioned elsewhere, Dewey insists that the very first of these is the instrumental nature of the child's acquiring, and of all that he acquires, for he acquires nothing in a vacuum, everything in what Dewey calls "the continuum of experience." And so the teacher cannot merely instruct, for in the whole of life there is no occasion within which mere information, divorced from use and the meanings of experience, appears as a motive sufficient in itself. The task of the educator is to provide experience. In order to do this, he must first *interact* with his students, not as a teacher, but as a person; for there is no other way to provide the second essential of experience, which is *continuity*. Dewey does not mean here merely the continuity of a curriculum, but the continuity of lives within which the school itself is but one of many functions. Now certain conditions are indispensable to interaction and continuity. If the teacher is to interact, he must know his students individually. But how can he know them unless they are free to reveal themselves, each one in his uniqueness? From considerations such as these follow the structure of the school. . . .

There are many reasons why Dewey's ideas are hard to realize. They are arduous and subtle even in the thinking (whatever may be said of the plain-pine Yankee homeliness of his style). They are especially arduous in the doing. Like Tolstoy, he understands method not as mere formal conception that antedates its own occasion, but as *what happens*. The so-called "methods" of education taught in our colleges cannot in fact be used. They are mere potentialities, are often impediments, and are worth nothing until they vanish and reappear again as technique. And technique cannot be taught, though it can indeed be learned. The reason is simple: each appearance of technique, each application, each solution, is unique. The work of the teacher is like that of the artist; it is a shaping of something that is given, and no serious artist will say in advance that he knows what will be given.

Dewey would certainly approve the suggestions made by Paul Goodman and Elliott Shapiro that group therapy be central to the training of primary teachers. The teacher's instrument is himself. Group therapy puts us in touch with ourselves. It clarifies emotions and reduces the blind spots in behavior. We cannot pass from the mechanical conceptions of method to the living reality of technique except by passing through ourselves.

Let me describe three of the deeper reasons why Dewey's thought is so hard to translate into action. It requires, first, that the educator be modest toward experience, modest toward the endless opening-outward and going-onward of life, for this going-onward is the experience of the young. Precisely this fact of life, however, evokes anxiety, sorrow, regret, and envy in the hearts of adults. It is not easy to give oneself wholeheartedly to the flow of life that leaves one, literally, in the dust. If we often scant the differences between the young and ourselves, and prefer the old way, the old prerogatives, the old necessities, it is because, at bottom, we are turning away at all times from the fact of death. Yet just this is what modesty toward experience means: a reconciled awareness of death. It is a difficult spiritual task; and it lies right at the heart of the educational function.

To be open to experience means, too, that we cannot repeat past successes with past techniques. We cannot organize the educational event in advance. Certainly we can plan and prepare, but we cannot organize it until we are in it and the students themselves have brought their unique contributions. And so there is a point beyond which our tendency to organize becomes inimical to experience, inimical to teaching. Much that belongs to teaching precisely *as* a profession is therefore inimical to teaching. Yet just this tendency to organize and to elevate the gratifications of the profession—the status of expertise, the pleasures of jargon, the pride of method—is composed largely of two things, both inescapably human and hard to transcend: anxiety and vanity. Here again, a difficult spiritual task.

Yet it may be that neither of these tasks amounts to quite the impediment to Dewey's thought that we find spread large in the social and economic structure of our country as a whole. In Dewey's conception, the vital breath of education flows to the schools directly from the community. The function of teaching arises in the community. The product of teaching returns to it. Writing in 1902, 1916, 1936, Dewey did not envision, and could not, the incredible consolidation of centralized power that has taken place in our country since World War II. Education must be *lived*. It cannot be *administered*. And we have become, as a nation, a wretched hog wallow of administrative functions. The hope that animates Dewey's educational thought, and that he stated in greatest detail in *Democracy and Education,* seems downright utopian today:

Character and mind are attitudes of participative response in social affairs . . . it means that we may produce in schools a projection in type of the society we should like to realize, and by forming minds in accord with it gradually modify the larger and more recalcitrant features of adult society.

What might Dewey today, with the degeneration of our social institutions well in mind, propose as the first task of education? It seems to me that he would be alarmed especially by the social effects that appear as individual traits, in some sense traits of character. The illiteracy of youths who were born intelligent, and who have been schooled, is the kind of individual collapse which, on the face of it, is a social effect. The distrust of adults now rampant among the young is a social effect (for it is profoundly unnatural). The savagery and violence of so many children in the slums; the passivity, the willingness to be bossed of so many children in the suburbs; the poor health (by world standards) of our young; the extraordinary increase in juvenile crime—all these are social effects. They are the handiwork especially of our politicians and educators, though obviously they are the product of our society as a whole. Dewey based much of his thought upon considerations of the fundamental human nature visible in the young. One of the remarkable facts of life (it is perhaps the only thing that saves us from ourselves) is that this indwelling nature, prior to its exposure to school and to the crushing effects of public life, reaches, in the vast majority of cases, a quite adequate development in the life of the home—reaches it in the most ordinary, routine, taken-for-granted way. (And this remarkable corollary needs to be stated: that after leaving the home, as a more or less total environment, the child will never again, in all his experience of professionals, experts, and trained personnel, encounter services as adequate to his own growth as were those of his mother and father, sisters and brothers, relatives and friends.) Dewey referred to this routine development of the child as the starting point of education. But it is a starting point that continues. It remains, through the whole of life, the only possible foundation for the educational function. Nothing can be added to it. Nothing should be subtracted. Growth and development are a shaping of powers that already exist. And so it seems to me that Dewey would tell us today that our first task is to recover this routine adequacy of the child, these ordinary human powers, from the neglect, abuse, and degeneration into which they have fallen. There is no other foundation upon which to build. In short, we cannot speak of teaching and learning at all unless we speak of ways and means of sustaining the powers that are visible in the child when first he comes to class.

§ THE PRACTICE of AFFIRMATIVE EDUCATION

Obviously, there are as many ways to practice affirmative education as there are classrooms that can admit innovation. We have seen thus far a foundation for a cohesive view of education, a redefinition of learning, a new look at what makes a teacher and a student, and new insights into what can take place in the experience we call education. We can now state certain general points:

1. Affirmative education occurs when students and teachers find each other and when learning emerges from mutual discoveries that are the result of that expanding relationship.
2. The content of learning is not the curriculum, the book read, or the course content; it is the learning process itself.
3. Discipline, course requirements, grades, and the like are all indications that the desirable educational experience may not be occurring.
4. Affirmative education is related to life experience; its method is to increase the degree of sophistication in problem-solving techniques.
5. Genuine encounter, emotional and intellectual, is the basis for a relationship between student and teacher.

For obvious reasons, the degree to which this view of education can find application depends on the particular school system and on the teacher's ability to transform himself. Affirmative education cannot become institutional policy; it can only be achieved by individual teachers who are willing to let their students learn how to teach themselves.

Putting affirmative education into practice is complicated by the fact that where real experimentation is going on it is not necessarily wise to report the findings publicly. For example, where community dissatisfaction with the school system is expressed, the atmosphere is ripe for experimentation, but hostile to publicity about the experiments. Some curricula, policies, and lesson plans are so stifling and regimented that those who depart from expected procedures can be quite vulnerable if they are not discreet. Then, of course, there are the practical limitations that hamper any attempt to innovate within the classroom: conservative colleagues, the time allotments given to any one teacher, the class size, and so forth.

Nevertheless, numerous experiments have been documented and there are some fully functioning schools where affirmative education is under way. In some cases, such as the Summerhill and Montessori methods, the concepts have become somewhat codified and, in any case, have been widely reported. I have chosen examples of affirmative education in practice and essays on the problems of putting the concept into practice from a wide variety of sources. Each selection suggests the spread of ideas about affirmative education and the diversity of their application.

In the first essay, Marie Muir describes the application of affirmative education on the elementary level in the English school system. Muir deals with a hostile question that is raised frequently by the deprecators of affirmative education: "If the teacher diminishes the structures in the classroom, won't the result be chaos?" Her essay is a balanced and cogent consideration of this problem. Kenneth Koch's description of teaching poetry to children may be thought of as a practical example of some of the insights found in Muir's essay. Koch finds that children do take responsibility for their learning, for there seems to be no shortage of enthusiasm for experiences that are the child's own. His essay also shows that the affirmative educational experience can be as meaningful and as full of learning for the adult teacher as it is for the child learner.

It may surprise some to find an essay on "relevance" coming so late in this book. However, its placement here may clarify the reader's perception of this often misused word. William Glasser's books *Reality Therapy* and *Schools without Failure* are partly based on his experiences teaching and working in the Los Angeles area. The selection included here is a reasonable and humane discussion of the need to integrate young people's experience outside the school with their experience as students. Many educators assume that school is the only place for youthful assembly and that the skills learned in school are distinct from those used outside the classroom. By relevance, Glasser means the employing of activities the students engage in voluntarily as a means for improving the skills that are being taught. Like many of our contributors, Glasser suggests we first find out how children behave and then use that behavior to promote learning.

The methods advocated in these three essays can be applied on the elementary and secondary school levels. Since affirmative education is a cumulative experience, one would expect its fullest expression to be realized in higher education. In "Survival University" John Fischer tells the story of an educational program that is attempting to synthesize all the elements of affirmative education into an integrated and significant educational experience. Gone are most of the fragmentations that show so clearly what is wrong with education today. In their place one finds a diffusion of the interface between life, education, relevance, commitment, and involvement. Learning and living come together in Green Bay through a format that not only provides personal growth but also is of positive value to society itself.

I have written a concluding essay for this section because I feel that much remains to be said. The main emphasis in the literature on affirmative education, both in this book and elsewhere, is on the interaction between students and teachers and between students and students. Questions of priorities, curricula, the learning process, course content, and so forth become central to the discussion. But if affirmative education is to be made available to the millions of students across this country, it must be noted that the educational environment itself must undergo drastic revision. Most existing classroom and school designs are antithetical to affirmative education, which therefore requires new structures, new spaces, and new opportunities within the educational environment.

It is unlikely that society will tear down buildings to provide better space for educational institutions. But it is not inconceivable that classroom design in the future can be based on more than economics and an obsolete concept of learning.

How Children Take Responsibility for Their Learning

MARIE MUIR

"What matters is not what we learn but how we learn it." This statement is familiar to those who discuss and read about contemporary developments in educational theory and practice and it seems relevant to the subject of responsibility for learning.

In the early days of English primary-school education, ends were (in official eyes at least) more important than means. Teachers were paid according to the results they obtained, not according to their methods of teaching. Results were assessed in terms of how much children had learned at regular intervals in their schooling, in the areas of reading, writing, and arithmetic. *How* this learning had been acquired did not seem to be a pertinent matter for investigation. In this century, and particularly in the past twenty years, the means by which learning has taken place are held to be at least as important as its end products.

Like most challenging statements, the one quoted here needs careful scrutiny. What children learn is never unimportant; but if we take the view that the attitudes, beliefs, and values that are learned during the years in school count for more than the facts acquired and memorized, if we think that the ability and the desire to go on learning beyond those years are valuable criteria of the worth of the educative process, then how children learn is inextricably bound up with what they learn. Thus, helping them to take increasing responsibility for their learning becomes a major consideration throughout their years in school.

Just to say that it is a good thing to make children responsible for their learning does not take us far. We have to determine what responsibility for learning involves and define the areas in which such responsibility seems appropriate. Do we mean responsibility for what to learn, how to learn, when to learn—or all of these? And what is the teacher's responsibility? In this chapter I shall describe under each of these headings the interpretation that a growing number of British primary schools are putting upon the concept of responsibility for learning.

RESPONSIBILITY FOR WHAT TO LEARN

Responsibility for what children learn in school (or perhaps it would be better to say "responsibility for what *can* be learned," because we are all aware that it is one thing to provide opportunities for learning certain things and another to ensure that these things are learned) has traditionally been shared by administrative bodies and teachers, in varying proportions. English teachers are fortunate in having a large share in this responsibility. The idea that children should be more than sleeping partners in the decisions that have to be made about the content of their learning is not new to educationists: it is implicit in doctrines of education through play, through interest, through experience —in any theory that postulates that children themselves are good judges of what they need to learn. Our nursery schools were the first part of the English educational system to put this principle into practice. Now, a growing number of infant schools for children aged five to seven years are paying increasing attention to this idea, and in recent years it has penetrated into our junior schools, for children of seven to eleven.

Responsibility for deciding what to learn takes different forms at different stages of the primary-school years. One condition is essential at all stages: there must be opportunities for choice in what can be learned, because none of us can exercise responsibility without choice. In English infant schools, opportunities for choice between different kinds of learning began in a small way. I remember my mother once telling me that the highlight of my own infant-school days (now fifty years behind me) was the occasion when I rushed home to tell her that a great treat was in store: on the following Friday afternoon we were to be allowed to choose between drawing with colored crayons and cutting out fancy doilies from newspapers. (She told me, too, how the agony of exercising this unaccustomed choice kept me awake half the night.)

From the 1930s on, some of our infant schools were including in their day a "basic skills" period that allowed children a certain amount of choice between reading, writing, and arithmetic. The same schools—and sometimes others—also introduced the "activity" period, in which the choice of what to do was defined not by the teacher but by the materials and equipment available in each classroom. The same years saw the introduction into a few junior schools of "centers of interest" or "projects" combining work in several subjects and pursued over a period of weeks or months, for part of every day or every week.

Responsibility for what to learn, in this kind of work, was usually shared by teachers and children: sometimes the choice was made by teachers, based on their knowledge of the interests and background of a particular class of children; sometimes content and organization were formulated by joint discussion between teachers and children, with children making the final decisions. This approach involved collective rather than individual responsibility.

Today, an increasing number of infant and junior schools are working along lines that encourage and develop individual responsibility for what is learned. Areas of choice have been widened in two ways: by the provision of a larger variety of stimulating materials that call for children's own decisions about how to use them and what to do with them, and by an increase in the proportion of time spent in school during which such choice may be exercised. New buildings planned to meet the new kind of organization contribute to this freedom, as well. A primary-school building that makes it possible for children and teachers to move from one activity to another or from one classroom to another with a minimum of trouble enables us to provide greater variety of activities. Thus, we can make more effective use of equipment and teachers' individual interests and contributions than in an older building, in which it is less easy to deviate from the "one class, one teacher, one classroom" idea. But, in old buildings as well as new, primary-school children now find opportunities for pursuing in their own way and at their own pace kinds of learning that traditionally have depended on teaching by adults rather than exploration by children; tables, corners, or alcoves are stocked with materials that invite handling, looking, listening, using, experimenting, and questioning.

Now, to choose what you do in school does not inevitably mean, of course, taking responsibility for what you learn. Before you can be responsible for something, you have to become aware of its nature and understand it. Children take time to become aware of "learning" as a conscious pursuit. In the earliest primary-school years, the kinds of learning that teachers wish to encourage often happen incidentally, in the course of pursuing other ends. For instance, the problems that face two six-year-olds using building blocks of various sizes to make a model garage can help them toward an understanding of the concept of area; attitudes of cooperation can begin to grow from the desire to accomplish something beyond the capacities of one seven-year-old on his own. But the extent to which these concepts and attitudes develop and are understood well enough to be applied to other situations depends on their teacher's ability to provide materials, suggest problems, and ask questions that encourage such development and understanding. It is difficult to say, therefore, that choosing what they do always results in children's taking responsibility for their learning. Sometimes they know not what they have learned until adults help them to relate particular instances to general principles. When, however, they begin to perceive what they need to know in order to solve new problems, to understand that trial-and-error is not the only nor the most effective way, and to appreciate that certain techniques and skills can make them increasingly independent of adult help, then responsibility for what they learn can become feasible.

A growing number of our primary schools now consider the fostering of this responsibility as one of their most important functions. This has meant a new approach to curriculum planning, to methods of teaching, and to resources for learning.

Children can exercise responsibility for deciding what to learn only if they are consulted in advance about the content of their learning—and only if the purpose of the proposed learning is explained to them. In schools that try to encourage this responsibility, we find frequent consultation between teachers and children about plans for future work. With the under-eights these consultations usually take place informally as teachers move around listening to and observing problems about current work and suggesting possible solutions and new developments to individual children or small groups.

As a result of these observations and discussions, from time to time, a teacher selects common difficulties or deficiencies and arranges a "helping time" for dealing with them or for sharing suggestions about further possibilities of extending work in hand. Helping times may be used to explain techniques of handling materials, suggest ways of finding out information, give information that is not available to children from other sources, or improve achievement in reading, writing, or mathematical skills. One helping time may be given to demonstrating different ways of making booklets, another to explaining the way in which reference books are classified in the class library, a third to giving the historical origins of a local event or visit, a fourth to demonstrating the way to use a simple dictionary to help with the spelling of unusual words.

Children are left to make their own decisions about whether to learn or not to learn what is offered in helping sessions. Those who choose to disregard these sessions are free to do so. It is thought that learning of this kind will not be effective unless or until children perceive its usefulness for themselves.

With junior classes (aged eight to eleven) joint consultation and decision-making take on a more formal aspect. Discussion centers around work for the next week, the next month or, sometimes, the next term. Children's suggestions for the content of future work are listened to, their views treated with respect; teachers encourage further suggestions by questioning, comment on the feasibility of proposals, point out considerations that children have failed to see or could not be expected to see for themselves, and make suggestions of their own. At times they will indicate that the proposed unit of work is too wide in scope to be tackled adequately in the time available: a proposal from nine-year-olds to study "All the inventions in the world" was narrowed down, during the course of discussion with their teacher, to the study of "The ten most important inventions in the world." (Choosing the ten proved to be a task that involved a high degree of responsibility!) Another time a teacher's contribution may help children to understand that the information available about a particular subject is insufficient to justify spending several weeks' work on it. "What it is like on other planets" comes into this category, although in the very near future this may no longer be true. Another teacher function is to help children to assess the comparative value of topics they have suggested. Recently, I listened to a group of ten-year-olds discussing the relative merits of "canals" and "famous battles" as topics for study and thought that the arguments put forth would have delighted the heart of a professional philosopher. Adult expectations about the content of learning and the requirements of the next stage in the education system are also factors that can be discussed and evaluated. The following comments recorded during a planning session with nine-year-olds illustrate that children who are treated as active partners in the business of learning rather than as passive recipients of its products are capable of appreciating and accepting that immediate interest is not the only consideration in deciding what to learn:

DANIEL: I think we should learn to do long division next.

GERALD: What's that?

DANIEL: Well, I don't know but they're always asking me at home if I have learned it yet. My brother can do it, so I expect I could if I tried.

AUDREY: How long would it take us to learn it, Miss X?

MISS X: I should think most of you would manage it in about two weeks, if you worked at it for a little while every day.

JOHN: Supposing we worked at it *all* day? Would we learn it in about two days then?

MISS X: I think you might get rather tired of it if you did it *all* day. Wouldn't it be better to do a bit each day?

GERALD: Oh no, if we really made up our minds we could do it all the time and learn it quickly.

CHRISTINE: What use is it—what do you do with it when you know it?

GERALD: I don't know, but I expect Miss X knows.

JOHN: Well, things you learn aren't always useful just when you learn them. Sometimes you have to wait and find out when they're useful.

ROBERT: Perhaps it's useful for when you do exams for 11+.[1]

1. The common phrase for the competitive entry to grammar schools at the age of eleven.

CHRISTINE: Is it, Miss X?

GERALD: I think we should find out all the things we should know for 11+, and make sure we know them, even if they are not very interesting. Then we shall see how much time we have got for interesting things.

Parents and teachers sometimes fear that children who are given a good deal of freedom about what they learn and how they learn it will neglect the fundamental skills of reading, writing, and mathematics. Sometimes schools that encourage initiative and choice in learning make a certain amount of work in these three areas compulsory, or try to use other activities to give meaning and interest to these three. But, in those primary schools where reading, writing, and mathematics are not unduly emphasized to the detriment of other kinds of learning this compulsion becomes unnecessary. Primary-school teachers no longer think that basic skills have to be learned first and then used to acquire knowledge or develop understanding. They find that children learn these skills more easily and effectively in the context of investigating aspects of their physical environment, recording those investigations, communicating their ideas and experiences to others, trying to find answers to the problems that they encounter from time to time. When children spend their school lives in an environment that offers intellectual, aesthetic, and physical stimuli and challenges, we find that some of them learn to read and to write and begin to comprehend mathematical relationships. Moreover, this learning happens in a way that requires little direct instruction from their teachers, and in what seems a minimum of time compared with that needed by children in schools where the three R's figure prominently in timetable and curriculum. Other children take longer and need more direction and individual help from their teachers. But when these children can see for themselves from the outset the context in which these skills are useful and illuminating, and when they are given the opportunity to experience the joy of successful learning in other directions before they begin on the mysteries, both literal and numerical, they settle down happily to the regular, consistent work necessary to become proficient readers, writers, and calculators. Extending the choice of what to learn does not detract attention and interest in what were once regarded as essential preliminaries to other kinds of learning; rather, it seems to enhance this attention and interest and to lessen anxiety about possible failures in areas of learning, which when compulsory tend to be accompanied in children's minds by fear of losing adult affection or approval.

The value of children's exercising some choice about what they learn depends largely on the possibilities of worthwhile learning open to them. In the past, the only choice often was either to learn what teachers decided to teach or to be thrown entirely upon your own resources in school. But primary-school teachers no longer look upon themselves as the sole or even the chief mediators of knowledge. For one thing, they now recognize that the kinds and extent of learning of which primary-school children have proved themselves capable are too many and too varied for any one adult to deal with adequately. For another, they and the children now have new media of teaching and learning at their disposal: books that children can use themselves, equipment for programmed learning, tape recorders, TV and radio sets, all of which contribute to an increasing diversity of worthwhile learning opportunities. The teacher's own personal resources of learning no longer define the area within which children can exercise choice: children can have direct access to reference information: books, catalogues of programmed learning units, details of forthcoming television and radio programs, lists of films and filmstrips. Study and discussion of all these sources provide new possibilities for learning as well as aids to pursuing subjects already chosen.

Deficiencies (real or imagined) in existing sources of learning sometimes provide an objective for a new unit of work. Recently, I observed a class where a group of ten-year-olds was organizing a "travel agency." This project involved, among other activities, compiling a series of travelers' guides for display and consultation. The children had visited the local public library to arm themselves with books useful for this purpose. Things went well until they found that there were no suitable books about one country on their agency's list. The first suggestion to meet this difficulty was that this country had better be omitted from the holiday attractions offered. Then one boy who had shown little inclination to contribute until that moment said firmly, "No, you can't leave it out just because there isn't a guide. That's the country we should write a guide to ourselves, if nobody can find out much about it." Accordingly, a new school-made guide was eventually presented with pride to the local library. Its compilation engaged eight children for about two hours a day, over a period of six weeks; it involved reference to adult books and publications, inquiries to an Embassy, finding and talking with people who had visited the country in question, and long discussion (amounting to heated argument at times) about what should be included in the guide. It is doubtful whether a teacher-initiated, teacher-directed study on the same subject, spread over an equivalent period of time, would have produced the quantity and quality of intellectual effort demonstrated here: the comparison of information from different sources, careful scrutiny of material collected, and almost passionate concern about the accuracy of the contents of the handbook, which was finally produced. It would have been equally difficult for any other course of study on the same subject to have resulted in the real thrill of achievement made manifest when the new guide was donated to the children's department of the local library and accepted to make good a deficiency in its own supply of books about other countries.

This example illustrates another aspect of responsibility involved in "choosing what to learn." Primary-school children are pragmatic creatures: they like to see a practical purpose for at least some of their learning. This pragmatism can take several forms, but one of the greatest inducements towards taking a responsible attitude toward your own learning is to be in a position of being responsible for what somebody else learns from you. Organizing an exhibition, giving a series of talks, making a book to be read and used by others—any of these results in concern about finding and giving accurate information, deciding what is essential and must be included, what is peripheral and may be omitted, investigating the reliability of sources and verifying facts, perceiving questions that cannot be answered as well as answering those that can. There can be no more intellectually valuable pursuits than these, and they seem to be more in evidence in this combination of learner-teacher role than in most other school situations.

RESPONSIBILITY FOR HOW TO LEARN

How children or adults learn is still something of a mystery, in spite of the years of experimental work. No one theory of learning seems to embrace all varieties of human activities that go on in the name of learning. To say that children themselves should take some responsibility for how they learn, therefore, seems rather a tall order. How to learn is not a conscious problem for children until they understand that not all the things they want to learn (or we want them to learn) can be acquired solely by exploration, by trial-and-error. When these methods which served well enough for most of their purposes in the preschool years fail in the face of new kinds of learning, children are bewildered and assume that some sort of magic accounts for the success others have achieved in these directions; they have only to find the right formula to break the spell, they think, and the secret will be theirs. "My daddy sits like this with his legs crossed, and he holds a book in front of him, then he can read it," a six-year-old told his teacher. "Well, I sit with my legs crossed, and I've held the book up like this for a long time but nothing happens. What must I say to the book to make it work?"

It takes quite a long time for most primary-school children to understand that there is no magic, that some kinds of learning do not suddenly reveal themselves to the initiated, that effort and practice are required from them and sometimes help from teachers. Only as they begin to realize this does how to learn become a meaningful problem.

Those of us who teach are tempted to think that it is our responsibility to solve this problem, as far as we can. So we study appropriate ways of presenting mathematics, natural science, or music to children at varying stages of development and with varying abilities, and when what we are trying to teach appears to have been learned, we feel that we have chosen successful methods. But our anxiety to teach well sometimes leads us to forget that learning is not a commodity to be handed over to the consumer already processed, packaged, and labeled but an activity, the nature of which can be communicated only by the initiated looking at the problems together with the uninitiated, investigating difficulties and discussing possible solutions rather than demonstrating and instructing.

This principle is well established at the highest levels of English academic education. Its relevance to the primary-school level is now beginning to be recognized. The following summaries of two class discussions (one in a class of ten-year-olds, the other with eight-year-olds) illustrate how some primary-school teachers now are attempting to help children toward an active responsibility for how they learn as well as for what they learn.

The previous week, after suggesting and considering with the teacher several possibilities for the next unit of work, the first class had decided to make a study of rivers. All those wishing to join in were asked to prepare suggestions about what this piece of work might include, how the study was to be made, and presented for discussion in this period.

After everybody had made their suggestions, a provisional list of those aspects of the topic it was thought useful or interesting to study was agreed upon. This was the list:

> How rivers begin and end
> Ways of traveling on rivers
> The most important rivers in the world
> Famous explorations of rivers
> River animals
> People who work on rivers
> Bridges

The teacher, Mr. H., then asked for ideas as to how they should set about this study. Not unexpectedly, the first proposal was that they should hire a boat big enough to take them all on a trip from the source to the mouth of the nearest river. The teacher pointed out that the practical possibility of this trip would depend on how long it would take, how much it would cost, and whether a suitable boat was available. Offers were made to investigate such matters as the length of the river in question, how much of it was navigable by a large vessel, and how many miles per hour it was possible to travel on a river; and they were accepted.

Mr. H. then asked if it would be better to make this trip, or as much of it as proved to be possible, right at the beginning of the study, in the middle of it, or toward the end. The subsequent discussion on the merits of observation before information versus information before observation would have done credit to some more professional investigators. Initially, majority opinion was in favour of starting off with the trip—"to see what we find"—but this was swayed by the comment, "We might miss some of the best things, if we didn't know they were there." But how would you find out, then, what not to miss? Well, you could ask people who knew. Did anybody know anybody who had journeyed all the way up and down the river? Nobody did. Then could we find people who knew parts of it well? How? Put an advertisement in the local paper, ask the police, and send a letter to all the parents associated with the school were among the suggestions offered here.

Other sources of information were then discussed. Somebody knew there was a Canal Museum; was there also a River Museum to write to or visit? Could we write to the BBC and ask if there were any television or radio program about rivers scheduled for the near future? Where could we find out about films or filmstrips? What kind of books should we look for in the school library and the local public library?

Everyone agreed that the subject of the tangible results of this piece of work—the production of books, friezes, models, the possibility of holding a River Exhibition—could be left to the next meeting. The question of how work was to be organized seemed to be more urgent. Should everybody set out to find out all they could about the topics chosen, or should there be division of labor among groups? Would it be best to have the same number in each group? Supposing nearly every class member wanted to join the same group? How would each group let the rest of the class know what it was doing? Should everybody produce his or her individual book about rivers, or should we aim at two or three books containing contributions from those who wanted to offer them?

Finally, Mr. H. said he would like to know what his function in all this was to be. It was made clear that he would be expected to suggest sources of information, help with difficulties, answer questions, and settle arguments.

The second example of the class-discussion approach involved eight-year-olds who had reached the stage of realizing that the speed of their numerical calculation was being slowed down by their having to work out some parts of the multiplication tables or look them up on a chart. Their teacher, Miss T., had suggested that it would be worthwhile to give some time to memorizing these tables, that there were different ways of doing this, and that it would be useful to exchange ideas and then let everybody make his or her plan of work for accomplishing this task.

Miss T. then asked the children to suggest the kind of problems they needed to think about in their planning, and from their suggestions and her questioning the following points were listed:

> How to identify those answers that you couldn't remember, or frequently got wrong
>
> Ways of helping yourself to memorize these answers
>
> How often it would be useful to practice them—and for how long at a time
>
> How to test your own progress

Each of these headings was discussed in turn. The first brought suggestions from the children for making their own individual lists of items they failed to recall or made mistakes about in the course of their work. One or two saw that there could be deficiencies in this system and put forward the idea of making a test by which all items could be checked. Miss T. said there were ready-made tests of this kind which she would make available. (But it was interesting later to find that most of the children preferred to make their own.)

Suggestions for practice methods fell into two categories: those that one child could use on his own, and others to be used by children joined together in pairs or small groups. These children had been accustomed to a good deal of choice about how they worked and with whom they worked, so from the beginning they assumed that everybody would tackle this particular learning problem on his own or with others, as he pleased.

The issue of how many items it was useful to try to memorize at a time was introduced here. Arguments for concentrating on one or two items or for spreading their attention over a dozen were put forward and considered in a way that would not have disgraced experimental psychologists who have interested themselves in problems of memorization. Plans for making simple games (mostly variations on the basic patterns of Bingo, Snakes and Ladders, and Snap) were discussed, and it was agreed that everybody should contribute toward a "lending library" of games useful for this purpose.

There was much difference of opinion about problems that we adults would have labeled *frequency and distribution of practice*. Some children advocated the policy of "the longer you spend on it, the sooner you will learn it." Others thought it likely you would get bored easily and waste time if you tried to do too much at once. At this point, the teacher indicated that for this kind of work adult experience on the whole supports the policy of "little but often" and suggested that a few minutes at odd intervals in each day might prove more profitable than half an hour at a stretch.

Ingenious suggestions for progress tests and methods of recording achievement were forthcoming, and several children undertook to incorporate these in a loose-leaf book, and they stated magnanimously,

"Everybody could borrow it, even if they haven't suggested anything for it." Perhaps the fact that none assumed the teacher would test progress was the most telling evidence that they themselves had accepted responsibility for this particular learning task.

There were times in the following two weeks when certainly this classroom could have been called a *learning laboratory*. Each child conducted individual experiments in memorizing multiplication tables, compared results, offered advice to others, checked his own progress, and dealt with his own difficulties. To an onlooker, it was clear that something of the involvement, interest, and satisfaction of achievement which we regard as characteristic of learning at its best had gone into what is for some children in other circumstances a boring mental chore. . . .

THE RESPONSIBILITY OF THE TEACHER

Helping children to accept and exercise responsibility for their learning does not mean that teachers abdicate *their* responsibilities. Like adults, children can be responsible only for what is within their capacity and control, and teachers must retain responsibility for determining the areas within which children's decisions are desirable and effective. Unless the adults with whom they learn set limits to these areas, children of primary-school age are likely to feel insecure. In order to experiment confidently and usefully with making their own decisions about what to learn, how to learn, and when to learn they need to know that in the background are adults who are willing to help but ready to point out considerations children may not be aware of themselves. Adults can help by preventing mistakes that might have serious consequences and if necessary should be prepared to uphold the needs of a minority against the wishes of the majority.

Sometimes, too, teachers make it clear that those who teach (as well as those who learn) need to establish certain conditions, if their work is to be productive. For instance, they will stipulate that if children choose to join a group for the purpose of learning a foreign language, they must work regularly with the group, because spasmodic attendance would make the teacher's task difficult and impede the progress of the whole group. They will insist, if necessary, that the principle of deciding for yourself *when* you want to learn has to be modified, if your activities interfere with other children's freedom of decision about when to learn, or if the cooperation of a number of children at the same time is essential to the work in hand. Playing orthodox or unorthodox musical instruments comes into the first category, dramatic work into the second.

It is in relation to *what* children learn that the responsibility of their teachers needs clear definition. If all kinds of learning were of equal value, no problem would arise: teachers could restrict their function to suggestion, approval, encouragement, and help with children's own proposals about the content of their learning. But the chief justification for providing special people, places, and times for the pursuit of education lies in the belief that some kinds of learning are more worthwhile than others. Many of us maintain that the most important function of education is to help human beings to discriminate between the worthwhile and the worthless, and although we do not wish to underestimate the importance of *how* we learn, we could not happily agree that *what* we learn does not matter.

Therefore, a teacher's responsibility lies in trying to ensure that the choice of what to learn is offered to children in the context of that which is likely to be of enduring rather than ephemeral value: learning that will add to new understanding of vital issues of human living on all levels, learning that will foster an appreciation of those intellectual and aesthetic disciplines that interpret and transmit the raw material of experience into arts and sciences. This task is not easy, because it involves sensitivity toward growing human beings plus an awareness of the nature of these disciplines. Mediating between these two calls for a constant consideration of priorities.

Teachers who work in the primary schools described in this book are aware of the difficulties of this responsibility but do not shirk it nor seek to throw off the burden it entails by adhering to the view that "children should learn only what interests them." Instead, such teachers share with their children the considerations that sometimes lead them to reject children's proposals for the content of learning.

Because they themselves have had experience with the difficulties as well as the satisfaction that responsibility brings with it, children are more ready to recognize the validity of the responsibility than are children from whom responsibility has been withheld on the grounds that they are not yet ready for it. Children are more ready to go along with adult authority when they have been given opportunities for testing adult suggestions and advice.

Wishes, Lies, and Dreams:
Teaching Children to Write Poetry

KENNETH KOCH

Last winter and the spring before that I taught poetry writing to children at P.S. 61, on East 12th Street between Avenue B and Avenue C
in Manhattan. . . . Unlike other special teachers, I asked the regular
teacher to stay in the room while I was there; I needed her help and I
wanted to teach her as well as the children. I usually went to the
school two or three afternoons a week and taught three forty-minute
classes. Toward the end I taught more often, because I had become so
interested and because I was going to write about it and wanted as
much experience as possible. . . .

Some things about teaching children to write poetry I knew in
advance, instinctively or from having taught adults, and others I found
out in the classroom. Most important, I believe, is taking children
seriously as poets. Children have a natural talent for writing poetry
and anyone who teaches them should know that. Teaching really is
not the right word for what takes place: it is more like permitting the
children to discover something they already have. I helped them to
do this by removing obstacles, such as the need to rhyme, and by encouraging them in various ways to get tuned in to their own strong
feelings, to their spontaneity, their sensitivity, and their carefree
inventiveness.

At first I was amazed at how well the children wrote, because there
was obviously not enough in what I had told them even to begin to
account for it. I remember that after I had seen the fourth-grade Wish
Poems, I invited the teacher, Mrs. Wiener, to lunch in order to discover her "secret." I thought she must have told her students certain
special things to make them write such good poems. But she had
done no more than what I had suggested she do: tell the children to
begin every line with "I wish," to not use rhyme, and to make the
wishes real or crazy. There was one other thing: she had been happy

and excited about their doing it and she had expected them to enjoy it too.

I was, as I said, amazed, because I hadn't expected any grade-school children, much less fourth graders, to write so well so soon. I thought I might have some success with sixth graders, but even there I felt it would be best to begin with a small group who volunteered for a poetry workshop. After the fourth-grade Wish Poems, however, and after the Wish and Comparison Poems from the other grades, I realized my mistake. The children in all the grades, primary through sixth, wrote poems which they enjoyed and I enjoyed. Treating them like poets was not a case of humorous but effective diplomacy, as I had first thought; it was the right way to treat them because it corresponded to the truth. A little humor, of course, I left in. Poetry was serious, but we joked and laughed a good deal; it was serious because it was such a pleasure to write. Treating them as poets enabled me to encourage them and egg them on in a nonteacherish way—as an admirer and fellow worker rather than as a boss. It shouldn't be difficult for a teacher to share this attitude once it is plain how happily and naturally the students take to writing.

There are other barriers besides rhyme and meter that can keep children from writing freely and enjoying it. One is the feeling they have to spell everything correctly. Stopping to worry about spelling a word can cut off a fine flow of ideas. So can having to avoid words one can't spell. Punctuation can also be an interference, as can neatness. Good poetic ideas often come as fast as one can write; in the rush to get them down there may be no time for commas or for respecting a margin. All these matters can be attended to after the poem is written.

Another barrier is a child's believing that poetry is difficult and remote. Poetry should be talked about in as simple a way as possible and certainly without such bewildering rhetorical terms as *alliteration, simile,* and *onomatopoeia.* There are easy, colloquial ways to say all these: words beginning with the same sound, comparisons using *like* or *as,* words that sound like what they mean. Poetry is a mystery, but it is a mystery children can participate in and master, and they shouldn't be kept away from it by hard words.

Again on the subject of language, the various poetry ideas should be presented in words children actually use. I don't think the Wish Poems would have been so successful if I had asked my students to start every line with "I desire." Nor would "My seeming self" and "My true self" have worked well in place of "I Seem To Be / But Really I Am." One should be on the lookout, too, for words and phrases that tell the child what to say and take him away from important parts of his experience: I think "make-believe" and "imaginary'" are such words.

When I told a teacher at another school about the "I wish" assignment, she said that she had done almost the same thing but it hadn't turned out as well. She had had her students write poems in which every line began with "Love is." I never heard a child say "love is" in my life, and so I wasn't surprised that they hadn't responded wholeheartedly.

One bar to free feeling and writing is the fear of writing a bad poem and of being criticized or ridiculed for it. There is also the oppression of being known as not one of the "best." I didn't single out any poems as being best or worst. When I read poems aloud I didn't say whose they were, and I made sure that everyone's work was read every so often. If I praised a line or an image I put the stress on the kind of line or image it was and how exciting it might be for others to try something like that too. That way, I felt, the talent in the room was being used for the benefit of everyone.

The teacher shouldn't correct a child's poems either. If a word or line is unclear, it is fine to ask the child what he meant, but not to change it in order to make it meet one's own standards. The child's poem should be all his own. And of course one shouldn't use a child's poetry to analyze his personal problems. Aside from the scientific folly of so doing, it is sure to make children inhibited about what they write.

A surprising discovery I made at P.S. 61 was that children enjoyed writing poems at school more than at home. I had assumed that like grown-up writers they would prefer to be comfortable, quiet, and alone when they wrote, but I was wrong. Once it had to be done away from school, poetry was part of the detestable category "homework," which cuts one off from the true pleasures of life; whereas in school it was a welcome relief from math, spelling, and other required subjects. Closing their heavy books to hear about a new idea for a poem made the children happy and buoyant. There was also the fact of their all being there in the room, writing together. No time for self-consciousness or self-doubts; there was too much activity; everyone was writing and talking and jumping around. It was competitive in a mild and exhilarating way: it was what everyone was doing, and everyone could do it.

The children wrote a few lines, showed them to each other, copied, teased, called to me for help or admiration, and then went back to their writing. Out of this lovely chaos, after fifteen minutes or so, finished poems would begin to appear, handed to me written in pencil on sheets of notebook paper, that would make me gasp. That is how almost all these poems were composed. The classroom was so drab-looking and noisy, with the students talking, the PA system going BOOP BOOP, and the trash can going BOOM (during many a writing session it was rolled in and out of the room), that I couldn't imagine sitting there and writing a poem. The children, however, seemed not to be distracted at all.

I let the children make a good deal of noise. Children do when they are excited, and writing poetry is exciting. I let them change papers and read each other's poems too. Sometimes in that maelstrom of creation one student's idea would seem so irresistible that another would use it. But not many lines were stolen, and the poetry thief always went on to something of his own.

One important advantage to writing in class was that I was there: before the children wrote, to explain and inspire; and while they were writing, to act as reader, admirer, and furnisher of additional ideas. It is true that I could have explained an assignment and let the children carry it out at home. What I couldn't have done was keep the new idea and their excitement fresh in their minds from noon till seven-thirty, or whenever they would sit down to write. For each poem I did certain things and gave certain examples to help make the idea clear and to put the children in the mood for writing. In giving the Color Poem, for instance, I asked them to close their eyes; then I clapped my hands and asked them what color that was, Almost everyone raised his hand: "Red!" "Green!" "White!" I asked them what color Paris was; London; Rome; Los Angeles. I told them to close their eyes again and I said certain words and certain numbers, asking them what color those were. The point was to get them to associating colors freely with all kinds of things before writing the poem. Almost always a part of my preparation was reading other children's poems aloud, and the effect of these was most vivid when the class wrote immediately after hearing them.

I could also be helpful to the children while they were actually writing. Often students got the feeling when they were about to start writing that they didn't really understand the assignment, so they would call me over to make it clearer. Sometimes a student would be stuck, unable to start his poem. I would give him a few ideas, while trying not to give him actual lines or words—"Well, how do musical instruments sound? Why don't you write about those?" or "What do you hear when you're on a boat?" Sometimes students would get stuck in the middle of a poem, and I would do the same sort of thing. Sometimes I would be called over to approve what had been written so far, to see if it was OK. I often made such comments as "That's good, but write some more" or "Yes, the first three lines in particular are terrific—what about some more like that?" or "That's not exactly what I meant. Turn it over; let's start again" or "I think maybe it's finished. What about another poem on the other side?"

So I was useful in the classroom for getting the children in a good mood to write and then for keeping them going. And they were useful to each other in creating a humming and buzzing creative ambiance. They helped and inspired each other as well by the poetry they wrote, which afterwards everyone could read or hear. I have already mentioned my practice of reading aloud to one class the poems of another. Once I had discovered the various good effects of doing this, it became an important part of my teaching.

By listening to or reading poems, children can become excited about writing and can learn new ideas and techniques. Aware of the value of poetry for inspiring and teaching poets, I looked around for the right poems to use at P.S. 61. It wasn't easy. The children responded to adult poetry with interest and intelligence; my grade-school students obviously enjoyed the work of even the obviously difficult modern poets I read to them—Dylan Thomas, Theodore Roethke, John Ashbery. But adult poetry—even that of Whitman and other apparently easier writers—was too distant from the way they thought, felt, and spoke to touch them in so immediate a way that they wanted to write similar poems of their own. A hasty look at and a long memory of poetry for children by adults showed me that it was not what I wanted either. It was too often condescending and cute and almost always lacked that clear note of contemporaneity and relevance, both in subject and in tone, which makes the work of a writer's contemporaries so inspiring to him. The best poems I found to read, finally, were those that the children at P.S. 61 were writing. I didn't have any that would serve until the fourth graders wrote their Wish Poems. When I saw these I decided to try them out on the primary class. It was my first visit to this class, in which the students were from six to eight years old.

I had really been delighted by these poems, but the response of the primary graders was even wilder and happier than my own. There were about forty of them, seated at their desks arranged in a large U-formation, all looking up at me and wondering what was going on. They hadn't seen a "poetry teacher" before. When I started to read the fourth-grade Wish Poems, it was as though they couldn't believe what was happening. Their secret thoughts and dreams, cast into verse, and being read to them in school by a smiling man! How could anybody have found out such things?

> I wish I could leap high into the air
> and land softly on my toes.
> I wish I could dance in every
> country in the world. . . .
> —Melanie Popkin, IV

> I wish I had a kitten to do my
> homework
> And a chimpanzee to do my
> housework. . . .
> —Ruby Johnson, IV

Within a few moments, first a few students and then the whole class was shouting "Yeah!" at the top of their lungs after every wish, that is, after every line of every poem. The commotion was tremendous. The fourth graders' poems really moved them, and they were bursting with ideas for poems of their own. I hadn't been sure that children so young would be able to write anything, but paper was passed out and they immediately wrote one-line Wish Poems (to warm up) and a little later they wrote longer ones. Their handwriting was clumsy and their spelling was uncertain, but what they had to say and how they said it were something else—

> I wish me and my brother and my
> friend Paul were birds. . . .
> —David Jeanpierre, I

> I wish I was soso, and I wish I was
> bobo too. I wish I was a book
> so the children could read me. . . .
> —Zaida Rivera, I

I read some fourth-grade poems to my other classes too, with equally good, if less extravagant, effects.

Once this got started I was reading poems from all grades to all other grades. The primary graders wrote the first Used To / But Now Poems, and children in the other classes were excited by lines like Andrea Dockery's

> I used to be a fish
> But now I am a nurse. . . .

Some children took over her idea and made something of it for themselves—

> I used to be a goldfish
> But now I am a girl. . . .
> —Lisa Smalley, III

or, in a crazier vein—

> I used to be a nurse
> But now I am a dead person

> I always was Mr. Coke
> But now I am Mrs. Seven Up. . . .
> —Thomas Rogaski, III

The younger children's feeling for physical transformation was doubtless the emotional source of these lines, but I think Andrea's couplet was the literary influence that made possible its expression. Often other children's poetry would not only excite my students and make them want to write but would also, as in this case, suggest particular techniques or variations on a theme. Of course these two effects aren't really separate, since an artist tends to appropriate to some extent that part of someone else's work which inspires him. I wasn't concerned that the children would slavishly imitate each other and so be constricted rather than instructed. I felt that my attitude toward their writing would help prevent that, as well as their own strong inclination to make things of their own.

It was soon clear that it wasn't copying that was going on but something more like the usual artistic process of learning through influence and imitation. The poetry written at P.S. 61 was their poetry, as twentieth-century American poetry is mine. When they were older, that larger literature would be theirs too, but now, though it interested them, it was too difficult and full of adult attitudes for them to feel close to it. The works of their exact contemporaries who were writing on the same subjects were another matter. Images, lines, and ideas in one poem, if they were good ones, carried by my voice across the room, would instantly begin to blossom in new places, changed by the personality of the writer, and usually just as fresh and new as they had been before. . . .

I was learning from their poems also. Having the children associate colors and sounds as preparation for the Color Poems and the Poems Written to Music was an idea I got from Mary Minns's poem and others like it. We were, the students and I, creating something like a literary tradition, and everyone could learn and profit from it. It was not only poems written for the same assignment that I read to my classes. Colors had turned up before the Color Poem, and I read some poems in which they had occurred when I presented that assignment. Sometimes it was just an interesting turn of phrase or kind of verbal music that I wanted my students to hear.

So hearing and reading other students' poems inspired the children, made them want to write, gave them new ideas. Having seen how the children were affected by these P.S. 61 poems, I thought harder about how to bring in some of the great poetry of the past and present so that they could learn from it and be inspired by it in similar fashion.

They were getting some knowledge of that poetry indirectly through me, since it was, after all, the substance of what I knew about poetry; but I wanted them to feel the force of a poet like Whitman or Wallace Stevens directly. My early classes at the school had shown me it wasn't enough merely to read them this poetry. But now I knew a few things from reading them their own poems: that they were particularly attentive to poetry just before they were going to write, and that if the poem I read had something to do with what they were going to write about, their interest in and absorption of it was increased—I thought this would be true even if the poem was a little hard for them.

So what I had to do was find poems or parts of poems that fitted in with my assignments, or else begin with a poet's work and find a way to make an assignment out of one of its characteristics. By reading or hearing the poet's work before they wrote their own poems on a similar theme, they could enjoy it and learn from it; some of its remoteness would be removed by its being a part of something they themselves were going to do. Wallace Stevens's "Bantams among Pine Woods" would be a part of one of their activities rather than something outside them which they were to analyze, appreciate, or describe. Just as it is easier and more natural for children to write as if they *were* the snow than it is for them to describe it, so it is easier for them to participate in a difficult poem (that is, enjoy it, get lost in it, be moved and influenced by it) than to describe or criticize it. . . .

The way of teaching I have described worked as well with so-called deprived or disadvantaged children as it had with others. The children I worked with who had problems in reading and writing were those in "N.E." [1] classes at P.S. 61 and some of the students in the writing workshops at Muse. The reason I say "so-called" is that the words *deprived* and *disadvantaged* may mistakenly be thought to apply to the children's imaginations and their power to create things. The tragedy—and for a teacher, the hope and the opportunity—is not that these children lack imagination, but that it has been repressed and depressed, among other places at school, where their difficulties with writing and reading are sometimes a complete bar to their doing anything creative or interesting.

They needn't be. Degree of literacy certainly makes a difference in a child's ability to write easily and confidently, but it does not form his imagination. The power to see the world in a strong, fresh, and beautiful way is a possession of all children. And the desire to express that vision is a strong creative and educational force. If there is a barrier

---

1. N.E. stands for "non-English speaking," a rather misleading administrative term. Children I taught in such classes could all speak English, and all except one or two "language learners" could write it, though often with some difficulty in grammar and spelling.

in its way—in this case it was writing—the teacher has to find a way to break that barrier down, or to circumvent it.

Since writing was the problem, I had them say their poems out loud. So that they would excite and inspire each other as much as possible, I had them compose their poems together. When we did these spoken collaboration poems, I would sit with from six to fifteen students around a table or in a circle of chairs. I would propose a theme, such as Wishes or Lies, and they would make up lines, which I would write down. When we thought we had enough, we stopped, and I read the poem back to them.

Often in the course of composition I read it back too, to reinspire the students and to show them where we were. I usually called on them in order, though occasionally I yielded to the irrepressible inspiration of someone who couldn't wait to tell me his line. I found writing—or even typing—better than using a tape recorder. The time it takes to write or type a line gives the children a chance to work a little more on their ideas. And when the work is read back, it sounds more like a poem because all the incidental noise (laughter, shouted comments) is left out.

These collaborations almost always made the children want to make up, and usually to write, poems of their own. Composing a poem together is inspiring: the timid are given courage by braver colleagues; and ideas too good to belong to any one child are transformed, elaborated on, and topped. Lies are particularly exciting in this regard, but Wishes, Comparisons, Noises, I Used To / But Now, and some other themes can also become exhilaratingly competitive—

> I wish I was an apple
> I wish I was a steel apple
> I wish I was a steel apple so when
> people bit me their teeth
> would fall out. . . .

So a subject is built up, starting with something rather plain and becoming deeper and more interesting in its elaboration. The teacher can help this process along by interposing questions: Any special kind of apple? Why? Are there any other fruits anyone would like to be? Hands. Shouts. "I want to be an orange!" (spoken with an air of great discovery and a feeling of creative power). How big an orange? "I want to be an orange as big as the school!" More hands. "I wish school was a big orange and New York City was a fruit store and my block was a pineapple." Excited by this atmosphere, and often having stored up ideas of their own which they are eager to express, children are willing to face even the uncertainties of writing.

It's understandable that children with reading and writing difficulties might be shy of being natural and spontaneous in school. Often what they say is "corrected" for what's wrong in it before what's good in it is acknowledged. That makes it not much fun to talk. To help them be poets, I did just the opposite. I immediately praised whatever it was that was imaginative or funny or anything in what they said, and let the mistakes fall where they would. If I didn't understand something I would ask, but I made it clear I wanted to know the exact word or meaning so I could get more out of the line. Once children sense a playful, encouraging, and aesthetic (rather than corrective) attitude in the teacher, they become less shy and more willing to take risks.

The speed with which "nonwriting" children can become excited about writing poetry was made very clear to me in working with Mrs. Magnani's fourth-grade "N.E." class. Ron Padgett came with me the first time I visited the class, and he, Mrs. Magnani, and I each worked with about twelve students. We had decided to do a Lie Poem Collaboration. Lying, for all its bad points in daily living, is a very quick way to the world of the imagination. It is also a competitive pastime. Like the Mississippi riverboat men in *Huckleberry Finn,* the children at P.S. 61 were eager to do each other one better, to tell an even bigger, more astonishing untruth: I live on the moon; I live half the year on the moon and half on the sun; I live on all the planets: January on Jupiter, March on Mars, December on the Planet of the Apes. Different kinds of lies could also please and astonish: I am ten years older than my teacher; I like school. These fourth graders, with just the slightest encouragement from us, began to create strange realities with great gusto. When we read the group poems back to them, they were very excited. At all three tables they demanded to write Lie Poems of their own.

Once the students began to write down their individual poems, there was terrible chaos, since they were bursting with untruthful inspiration, eager to write, and unable to spell half the words they wanted to use. All the time they were writing, there would be a few students, frantically excited, shouting at me at the head of the table. I couldn't tell them, as I had told children in other classes (and even there not always with success), just to write the word any way they could, that spelling didn't matter, I would understand it anyway. They knew perfectly well they couldn't write it at all, and I knew I wouldn't be able to tell January from an elephant if I didn't show them how the words were spelled. Showing turned out to be better than telling. I had paper in front of me, and when they asked me a word, I wrote it down—rather, I printed it—as fast as I could. Telling them how to spell all the words would have taken forever, since no one could hear anything I said. It is tiring to work at the center of an inspired mob, and also rather heady. The noise and the activity had other values for the children: they were part of an excitement which enabled them to forget their "illiteracy" long enough to write poetry.

Another cause of the high spirits of this class was my asking them to put some of their lies in Spanish. I thought their knowledge of a second language was clearly an advantage, and I wanted them to know it. They liked using Spanish, and they also enjoyed translating for me when I didn't know what they had written. The mere fact that a word or phrase was in Spanish made it interesting and amusing to them. They all spoke English, but English was the language of the school, whereas Spanish was a kind of secret. Very few could write Spanish, in fact, so those who could helped the others to spell Spanish words as I was helping everyone to spell English ones.

After this beginning in which the children had spoken and written Lie Poems they were excited about poetry, and though spelling problems remained they went on liking to write it. They wrote a good deal. Like everyone else's poetry, theirs became richer and freer as a result of the poems they listened to and those they wrote themselves. . . . As in groups of good readers and writers, some children with writing problems are more inclined toward poetry than others; and some who can hardly write are more imaginative poets than many who write without mistakes. What seemed most important was that, of the children I taught, every one had the capacity to write poetry well enough to enjoy it himself and usually well enough to give pleasure to others, whether it was entire poems or surprising and beautiful images, lines, or combinations of words.

The educational advantages of a creative intellectual and emotional activity which children enjoy are clear. Writing poetry makes children feel happy, capable, and creative. It makes them feel more open to understanding and appreciating what others have written (literature). It even makes them want to know how to spell and say things correctly (grammar). Once Mrs. Magnani's students were excited about words, they were dying to know how to spell them. Learning becomes part of an activity they enjoy—when my fifth graders were writing their Poems Using Spanish Words they were eager to know more words than I had written on the board; one girl left the room to borrow a dictionary. Of all these advantages, the main one is how writing poetry makes the children feel: creative; original; responsive, yet in command. . . .

The change in the children is the most evident, but the teachers have changed too. Once they saw what the children were doing, they became interested themselves. They have given their own poetry writing assignments, they put children's poems on bulletin boards along with their artwork, and they have the children read their poems in class and in school assembly. Before, I think, poetry was kind of a dead subject at the school (dormant, anyway). For all their good will, the teachers didn't see a way to connect it with the noisy, small, and apparently prosy creatures they faced in the classroom. But now they have seen the connection, which is that children have a great talent for writing poetry and love to do it.

Relevance

WILLIAM GLASSER

In this [essay] I shall discuss relevance and its relationship to school failure. Perhaps the best way to introduce the subject is to describe a class meeting about reading held with sixth-grade students at the 75th Street School, my home base in the central city of Los Angeles. On the edge of Watts, the 75th Street School is a 1900-student elementary school with all of the problems associated with a large school housed in an inadequate building. The students discussing reading had held many previous class discussions and were well versed in this technique. . . . Basically it is a method to get a whole class involved in thinking seriously about some important topic. The discussion was started with the question, "What is reading?" After a shaky beginning, because this was a new type of question to them, the students said that reading is what you do in school. You read your reading book silently or out loud, you read social studies books, science books, health books, and other school textbooks. Occasionally you go to the school library and you read *in class* some of the books that you take from the library. Although you sometimes take the library books home, you do so in relationship to school. The class also discussed the importance of reading and established that reading is vital because there would be much reading later in junior and senior high school, and the better you learned to read, the better you would do later.

I then posed the question, "Is reading important for anything besides school?" Further, I asked, "What would you do if the teacher gathered all the schoolbooks from every student in the class and said that from now on the only reading would be from material brought into the class by the children themselves?" I explained that the children would have to obtain written material outside of school and the school library and bring it to class to use as the school texts. The second question produced confusion. Many children thought I had proposed an impossible situation; without schoolbooks to read, school

"Relevance." From William Glasser, *Schools without Failure* (New York: Harper & Row, Publishers, Inc., 1969), pp. 45–58. Copyright © 1969 by William Glasser. Reprinted by permission of the publishers.

could not go on. More discussion followed of reading outside of school; some students did some outside reading, but not much. I was trying to get at whether or not they knew of the existence of important reading material away from school. Did they understand that the skill of reading could be used in their lives outside of school? After more discussion, they brought up the community library, but admitted that this was more in the nature of a right answer; for the most part, the library was also associated with school. Finally, I was able to separate them from school reading and its first cousin, library reading, by asking, "If you were given five dollars and told to buy a book, where would you buy it?" This question produced even more confusion, partly because no one in the class had ever bought a book (itself not unusual, as few sixth graders buy books) and partly because of their lack of knowledge about the whole process of buying books and of using money to buy a book to read. Most of them knew that bookstores existed, but only one or two had ever been in one. They had never thought that they might use a bookstore themselves later in their lives. Again, books were strictly associated with school.

The question about buying a book led to a discussion on reading materials in their homes. Where did these materials come from? Was there anything worth reading at home, anything that seemed important to them? Part of the difficulty of the discussion was that it was held at school; the children were totally oriented to the too common idea that what was discussed in school should have to do only with school. It was hard for them, in school, to think about reading at home. Eventually, we got into a discussion of the various reading materials in their homes. Magazines, newspapers, cookbooks, Boy Scout manuals, the Bible, and other material associated with home reading were generally available. When I asked them what their mothers and fathers read, they said, "The newspaper." Yet when asked why their mothers and fathers read the newspaper, they did not know. Most of the children had no interest in the newspaper and didn't understand why their parents seemed to read it with such interest. A few glanced occasionally at the sports pages, about one-half at the comics, but for most of the class the newspaper was something that existed for reasons unrelated to their lives.

I noticed that one boy sitting next to the teacher whispered something to her and then raised his hand. When I called on him, he said that he read comic books. I asked him if he enjoyed the comic books and he said that he did, very much. Joining in with some enthusiasm, the class revealed that almost everyone read comic books, traded comic books, and even bought comic books at the neighborhood grocery store. They were definitely of interest to the class. I then asked them, since comic books were so interesting, whether they brought them to school to read. They said they did once in a while, but they had to be careful; there seemed to be an unwritten school rule against comic books. Some teachers (although not their own) took away comic books when they found them. Because comic books were scarce and the money to buy them was scarcer, the children were wary of bringing them to school where they might be confiscated. I asked why in the world the school would want to confiscate the comic books. The children replied that comic books were bad; they were bad because they were nonschool reading and had nothing to do with school. The children had adopted the moral equivalents *good* and *bad* for certain types of reading. Comic books were classed as immoral. Later, I found out that the boy who had first mentioned comic books had received whispered permission from his teacher to talk about them. He didn't want to mention them to me, in school and in front of the other teachers watching the group meeting, unless it was okay. The discussion ended shortly after I found this enthusiastic use of reading. These children had spent six years in school. On the one hand, what they read with most pleasure outside of school was not accepted by the school. On the other hand, what they read in school, mainly textbooks, was not related to their own world outside of school. Textbooks were only accepted and understood as they pertained to the limited world of the school, present and future.

To me, this dichotomy in the attitude of the children is a serious problem, clearly pinpointing one of the two aspects of relevance in the school. Supposedly, we go to school to learn skills to use in our lives outside of school, but the only association these sixth graders had outside of school with the most important skill they have learned, reading, was either negative (for comic books) or nonexistent (for everything else). In other words, their work in school was completely separated from their world outside of school. They believed either that reading was irrelevant to their world or, when it was relevant, it was wrong.

It is against this background of the relevance of school to life that we can better understand the reading problems of these ghetto children and other children as well. School education has become, for many, an end in itself. A major purpose of learning to read—enjoyment—is reached only through comic books by the children in the discussion group and, I presume, many others in the area. We refuse to see that for many, perhaps most, of the children in the central city, reading does not lead anywhere. And as most schoolbooks are dull, dry, and unemotional, reading stops in school at a level far below that needed for the enjoyment of books beyond comic books. Children need the stimulation of reading outside of school; but because they do not see the relationship between school reading and outside reading, and because schoolbooks are themselves relatively unstimulating, many children never learn to read well enough to enjoy anything beyond comic books. *They miss the whole point of learning to read!* Unless children can be taught with books in school that have the same appeal as the barred comic books, and unless some way is discovered to bring nonschool books of equal appeal into the children's homes, for many children reading will never be more than a school activity.

In addition to reading, the most important subject in elementary schools, we must attempt to relate every subject taught—arithmetic, social studies, science, health, and even spelling and handwriting—to something that the children do in their own lives outside of school. *When relevance is absent from the curriculum, children do not gain the motivation to learn.* As more complex studies come along in later years of school, subjects that only motivated students can master, the children stand still—and they fail. We cannot depend upon the natural curiosity of children to bridge the relevance gap because too often it fails to do so, especially among children whose backgrounds and interests are different from those of their teachers. It is much easier for a middle-class teacher to teach relevance to middle-class students than to ghetto students whose world she does not understand. She too often tries to fit her students into the mold of her own life rather than attempting to fit her teaching to their world. I am not saying that we must have teachers whose background is the same as the children's, but teachers must learn to teach more than what is important to them in their own lives.

Teachers are also handicapped by the almost universal use of textbooks and their belief that they should rely heavily upon them. Reading texts in primary grades are written for a narrow stratum of middle-class children who came from intact homes with no obvious problems, an unreal condition for half the middle-class children and for almost all the ghetto children. Although some new texts do show a few Negro faces, they are merely the counterparts of middle-class whites, a meaningless change. A better procedure would be to eliminate texts altogether and have each school district select books from the large variety of relevant, low-priced paperbacks now widely available. Paperbacks are cheap, they can be taken home, they are expendable, and they can be changed as needed to insure their relevance. The widespread use of paperbacks by the schools would provide an incentive for book publishers to privide more and better paperbacks at lower prices. When texts are necessary, they should clearly relate to the child and his world. To summarize the first part of relevance, then, schools usually *do not teach* a relevant curriculum; when they do, *they fail to teach the child how he can relate this learning to his life outside of school.*

The other side of the coin, the second part of relevance, can be explained with the example of a second class meeting held with fourth graders in a suburban school. The fathers of the children were successful professionals or managers. Advanced degrees were commonplace among the parents, and education was highly prized in most of their homes. In contrast to the students in the 75th Street School, who had had many class meetings, these fourth-grade students had never before participated in a discussion of this type. The discussion was held in front of a large group of teachers because it was a demonstration meeting and, as it was evening, many of the parents of the children were in the back of the audience. The children soon become involved in these meetings so that the audience has no significant effect.

I started the discussion with the question, "What do teachers want from children in school?" After some initial hesitation, the group responded that teachers want children to learn, to do well, to get good grades, and to go on to college. The children were repeating all the cliché answers that they had heard from their parents and their teachers for so long. As I stated my questions more clearly, however, asking what the teachers want from children every day, they said that the teachers want answers. In response to, "Answers to what?" the children said answers, both oral and written, to all kinds of questions that teachers pose. Because I was pursuing a particular course, I asked the children to discuss the kinds of answers teachers wanted. Did the teachers want any particular kind of answer? After a few hesitations and a few false starts, one of the children answered, "Yes, what the teacher wants is right answers." When I followed with, "Do you mean that the questions asked are questions that can be answered by a right answer?" there was general agreement that they were. I then asked them, "Can teachers ask questions that do not have right and wrong answers but that still can have important answers?" This question threw the students completely off balance and they were unable to recover for the rest of the discussion. Despite much talk, no satisfactory response emerged. Because I was in a teaching situation and because we were in school, the students' orientation was almost totally to right and wrong answers. One boy, however, said, "Do you mean questions we give our opinion on?" When I asked him to continue, he said, "Well, do teachers ever ask questions that call for the opinions of the students in the class?" He thought for a while, and the others thought for a while, and they decided that what they thought—their opinions, their ideas, their judgments, and their observations—was rarely asked for in class.

I was asking, and they understood this very well, not for answers in terms of a first-grade "show and tell" session—what we did at home or what we did on vacation—but for answers that demanded an opinion of their own. Puzzled by my approach, because opinion questions had almost never been asked of them at school, they were reluctant to explore the subject further because they didn't think that their opinions were a proper topic for a school discussion. My question should have stimulated much more discussion than took place that evening. Their reluctance to talk about their interests, their ideas, their feelings, and their opinions was obvious as they shifted uneasily in their chairs, looked questioningly at each other, and generally showed signs of acute discomfort. Placed in a situation for which they were unprepared, they had almost nothing to say. They did not believe that their opinions—what they bring from their world to the school—are important in education. They could not see the connection between their own ideas and a discussion in school. Their own opinions, ideas, and judgments had not been sought for during the four years they had been in school, and they had no reason to think that they ever would be. The principal, sensing that the children were finally getting the point, went into their class the next day to continue the discussion. She said that she got an avalanche of response from the children as they began to understand that what she wanted was their honest opinion to an open-ended, non-right-answer question. Fast and furiously, as she tested one topic after another, they gave opinions on parents, teachers, homework, grades, and the world situation.

Here we can see the other side of the coin of relevance. School should be a place in which children can express their own ideas, based on their observations and experiences, and gain satisfaction from knowing that the school is interested in what they have to say. For at least five years these bright, eager, alert fourth graders hardly ever considered the possibility that school was a place for ideas and opinions generally, and especially for their own ideas and opinions. It was a place to learn the facts, to study the accepted and noncontroversial ideas of others. What they had to contribute, what they brought from their world, was not valued in school.

Thus we have both parts of relevance:

1. Too much taught in school is not relevant to the world of the children. When it is relevant, the relevance is too often not taught, thus its value is missed when it does exist.
2. The children do not consider that what they learn in their world is relevant to the school.

Relevance, the blending of one's own world with the new world of school, was poorly established for the students in the second example and probably is poorly established for most students. The class even seemed a little annoyed with me because I suggested that their opinions might be important in school. They really thought it was wrong, almost in the same way that the students in the first example thought that reading the comic books was wrong. It's bad enough that the schools do not relate what is taught to the children's world and that the children do not relate what they learn in the world to school. But the wall of irrelevance is built even higher by the idea that what the children learn or do in their world is in some degree wrong as compared with what they learn or do in school.

In addition, the children in the second class were annoyed because I suggested that they stray from the safe, familiar, easy path of right answers to a much less familiar path of ideas and opinions. The motivating power of relevance had been effectively crushed. Secure in the world of school with its right answers and relatively easy school work, they did not want to relate their own lives to school because it might not be so easy. Of course, these bright children in a good suburban school were not nearly the problem that teachers encounter in the central-city schools. The children do have problems, however, although they are usually not serious enough to move many complacent suburban educators toward new ideas such as classroom meetings. The educators blame parents for children who do badly; parents accept the blame and, in some cases, take the children to psychiatrists, a fact I am aware of through long personal experience.

Most of these bright students learn the right answers easily, get good grades on the tests, and go quickly toward higher education. Unfortunately, these same bright students are now creating problems on most college campuses, demanding, among other things, that relevance be brought into their education. Recently, a poll was taken at San Fernando Valley State College, a large state college on the outskirts of Los Angeles. The main dissatisfaction the students had with the curriculum was that it was not relevant to their lives. Almost 60 percent of the students said that they could see no relationship between what they were doing in school and what they expected to be doing later on. They were bitter and complaining about this lack of relevance. If the anger on our college campuses seems out of proportion to what seem to be the problems on the campuses themselves, I suggest that the anger stems not merely from the irrelevance of the students' college education but also from their sudden realization that all of their educational experiences from the first grade on have been irrelevant. The anger is now bubbling up from the depths of these many years of educational frustration until it erupts in college. Students have a right to a relevant education. If we attempt to teach them too many subjects unrelated to their lives, they will invariably lose interest and begin to fail. In addition, we err seriously if we take for granted that students can see the relevance in certain material just because we can. *I suggest, therefore, that the teaching of relevance itself be part of education.*

The relevance of some material is obvious. To little children, learning to read and to do arithmetic is important. But they soon rebel against reading and doing arithmetic which they cannot relate in some way to their lives. If we can do nothing more, we should explain to children that what they are learning is a part of general knowledge that has been found to be valuable; that if they do not see its immediate importance, they must accept on faith its importance to their general education. We should also be honest and say that certain subjects are taught only because the students will be tested on these subjects by the state or for entrance into college. When subjects are in the curriculum for reasons that we as teachers do not understand ourselves, we should tell the students so and explain that we are required to teach these subjects anyway. If we have to continue to teach irrelevant material, this explanation will work to some extent. Honesty is a fairly good motivator if the teacher has a good relationship with her class, if her class is fairly intelligent and sensitive, and if she is able to introduce some relevant material through the use of class meetings and discussions. But honesty by itself won't work forever, or for a curriculum overloaded with irrelevance. We must revamp the curriculum or we will sooner or later lose the students. They won't learn what makes no sense to them, and even if they would, it would be a waste of time.

Working recently with a group of fifth graders, I asked them what they were studying in mathematics. The purpose of my questioning was to test for relevance and to find out whether or not they were learning what the teacher was attempting to teach. When the class said that they were learning Roman numerals, I asked them what use there was in knowing Roman numerals. After a long discussion, we could arrive at nothing more than that Roman numerals were used to number chapters in some books. Nevertheless, the class felt that they should learn them because they were taught by their teacher, an excellent teacher with whom they were closely involved. In my desperation to try to get the class to think about the relevance of what they were learning, I asked, "Do they use Roman numerals in Rome?" Brightening considerably, the class decided that if Roman numerals were used in Rome, it might be a good idea to learn them; they would then be prepared if they ever went to Rome. This seemingly good idea did not last long, however, because one boy had been to Rome the previous summer. He told the class that, all the time he had been there, he had never seen a Roman numeral. The class was upset by this unexpected information, although the teachers thought it very funny. This example was not presented to put the teacher on the spot. The lack of relevance in the mandated curriculum is not up to her; she is required to teach these subjects whether she wants to or not.

Although knowing Roman numerals may have some use, there is no reason to test and grade students on this kind of knowledge. In trying to use grades to force students to learn irrelevant material, we succeed only with those who are generally successful. It works just the opposite for the failures. We should attempt to break down the wide disparity between school material and the outside world. Children are stimulated by material on radio and television and occasionally by newspapers and magazines. The writers of this material would fail if it were totally irrelevant. The school should use the popular media and relate them to the school curriculum. Magazines, newspapers, and television programs should be used as an aid, not condemned or disregarded because they are considered antagonistic to education.

A serious failing in most school materials is that the emotion has been completely drained out of it. Emotion helps the child see the relevance of what he is studying. Most school materials have little or no respect for the children's culture, especially for its rich emotional content. Too much school material is unrealistic, unemotional, and dull. Unless school materials are changed, failures will increase because children seem unable to get started without the emotional bridge to relevance. Not only is emotion necessary in the school material, but emotion itself, so important in children's lives, should also be present in class. Laughter, shouting, loud unison responses, even crying, are a part of any good learning experience and should be heard from every class. A totally quiet, orderly, unemotional class is rarely learning; quiet and order have no place in education as all-encompassing virtues. To the degree that I have seen them practiced, they do more harm than good as they increase the gap between the school and the world.

Survival U

JOHN FISCHER

If a 1965 graduate were to return today to Harvard—or Berkeley or
Kent State—he would have no trouble in recognizing the old place. In
spite of the years of protest, demonstrations, riot, and arson, he would
find that most of the old courses still are being taught in the same old
way, by the same professors, and often from the same lecture notes. So,
too, at nearly all of the long-established universities. Close scrutiny
might reveal a few changes around the edges: students added to some
committees (but not those dealing with faculty hiring and salaries),
ROTC courses abolished, government research curtailed, black studies
added, and probably a new president. But underneath the cosmetics,
the bone structure of the university, the traditional departments, remain much as they were fifty years ago; and the basic decisions still are
being made, as always, by the senior faculty.

Ten years from now, in the old universities the situation is likely to
remain much the same. For they are like the Galápagos tortoises: slow-
moving, shell-encrusted survivors from an earlier epoch, whose evolu-
tionary adaptations can be measured only on a geological time scale.
The more I see of American academic life—and I have been seeing a
good bit during the past decade—the more sympathy I feel for the
frustrations and impatience of the undergraduates. Though I feel no
sympathy at all for their occasional outbursts of violence, which are as
futile as kicking a Galápagos tortoise: they may break a toe, but they
don't change the nature of the beast.

Consequently, I have become convinced that any early and significant reform of American higher education can be hoped for, not in
the established universities, but only in the new ones that are being
started here and there throughout the country. In July 1969, I reported
here on the innovations which are being attempted at the new campus
of the University of California at Santa Cruz—an institution founded
on a fresh, though by no means revolutionary, concept of education.

"Survival U" by John Fischer. From *Harper's Magazine*, September, 1969, pp. 20,
22–23, 26–27. Copyright © 1969 by Minneapolis Star and Tribune Co., Inc. Reprinted by permission of the author.

Then in September 1969, I suggested a more radical departure: a Survival U, where all work would be focused on a single unifying idea, the study of human ecology and the building of an environment in which our species might be able to survive.

At the time, I supposed such an institution was wholly imaginary, if not utopian. So, apparently, did most of my readers. That column resulted in more correspondence than anything I have written, and was more widely reprinted.

To my embarrassment, I discovered a little later that a real Survival U had opened its doors in 1969, after three years of intensive planning. I had never heard of it, and even now it seems to be almost unknown throughout the rest of the academic world. Recently I spent several days there, talking with its students, faculty, and administrators—and I came away persuaded that it is the most exciting and promising educational experiment that I have found anywhere. If I were about to start to college, it would be my first choice—ahead of anything in the Ivy League or even Santa Cruz, which in comparison seems like a rather self-indulgent ivory tower in the redwoods.

It is a new campus—or rather a cluster of four campuses—located in and around Green Bay. Officially it is part of the much-troubled University of Wisconsin system; but in almost every aspect it is light-years away from anything ever tried before, in Wisconsin or anywhere else. It is a truly radical innovation, not only in purpose but in its internal structure and methods of teaching. Among other things, it is trying to break down the hegemony of the traditional disciplines—economics, political science, English literature, chemistry, sociology, and all the rest—which have imposed such a rigid pattern of departmental organization on the conventional universities. If Green Bay succeeds (an open question, since it is still in a precarious formative stage), it just might show the way for higher education to bust out of its Galápagian shell and sprout wings.

Like the imaginary Survival U, Green Bay is trying to focus all of its studies on a single overriding subject: ecology—that is, the environment we live in, both physical and social. Only recently, and perhaps too late, many of us have begun to realize that this is *the* cardinal subject. For unless we learn, pretty fast, to live on the earth's thin crust without destroying it, all the other subjects—from philosophy to twelve-tone music—will not only be irrelevant, they will simply disappear, along with *homo nonsapiens*. (If anyone is still skeptical about this dire fact, he would do well to look at the recent writings of Paul Ehrlich or René Dubos or the latest book from America's only scientist-poet, *The Invisible Pyramid* by Loren Eiseley.)

Moreover, in its broad sense ecology embraces all other subjects. The places where a man works and sleeps are part of his environment, just as the air he breathes and the sounds he hears, including both motors and Mozart. Whether this environment is good or bad depends on many things—economics, engineering, government, and geography, to begin with. Even international relations, since war could be the ultimate destroyer of the environment. Understood in this way, as it is at Green Bay, ecology is not simply one academic subject among others. It becomes an approach to all learning, a framework for organizing every field of study. . . .

To head the new institution, the state chose Edward W. Weidner, a man with a rare combination of talents. He is an academic administrator with imagination, the courage to strike out in new directions, organizing ability, and a knack for persuading others to go along with his ideas. . . .

Next to the emphasis on ecology, his most daring innovation is his break away from the sacrosanct departmental structure. At conventional universities this structure, along with the tenure system, is the flintiest obstacle to change.

Usually each department—Romance Languages, say, or History, or Architecture—has a customary number of job slots, most of them filled with tenured faculty members who cannot be fired. Since they choose the new men entering the department and decide who shall get tenure and when, old ideas tend to be perpetuated from generation to generation. Even the most ambitious and fresh-minded university president can do little to change these moated duchies; neither can he take much money away from their budgets to start something new. If he wants to experiment with black studies, or an institute of urban affairs, he has to find new money from the outside—a tough proposition in these days of shrinking appropriations and alumni contributions. Moreover, he cannot count on the support of the entrenched faculty for any innovation he attempts. Their first loyalty runs not to him or even to the university, but to their own disciplines and to the departments where they are practiced. The way to get ahead in their world is to write research papers or books which will establish them as Coming Men in their fields, and thereby win them offers of better jobs at more prestigious institutions. Often they don't give a damn for the university where they happen to be at the moment, much less for the students they are supposed to teach. And they may see any innovation as a threat to the relative importance of the old departments, a drain on money which might otherwise have gone to them.

A distinguished dean of a major state university recently remarked to me that "any real reform of higher education has to begin with abolishing the tenure system." That, he added, is almost impossible because the professoriat would fight it to the last drop of blood. He did, however, think that a start might be made by hiring new faculty members on five-year contracts, subject to renewal, rather than giving them permanent tenure.

"Would you like to write an article about that?" I asked.

"Good God, no," he said. "My colleagues would never forgive me. Besides, I'm on tenure myself. To be consistent, I would have to give it up—which I'm not about to do."

Weidner has not been able to escape the tenure system and its accompanying incubus, the compulsory Ph.D. union card, since they are built into the University of Wisconsin network, including Green Bay. But he has been able to sidestep (so far, at least) most of their evil consequences.

Because this university is new, it has been able to hire tenured professors who are young, enthusiastic, and daring enough to take a chance on an experiment which ignores the safe, worn ruts of academic advancement. In choosing them it has, in Weidner's words, had "little concern with the field of a professor's Ph.D. . . . but much concern with the kinds of ecological problems on which he wishes to focus, along with students and members of the community." (That last, seemingly perfunctory phrase conceals an explosive idea, to be noted in a moment.)

In addition, Green Bay foils the tenure system by means of "lectureships"—job slots in which it can place anyone whose experience is useful, even though he hasn't got a Ph.D. or climbed the prescribed rungs of the academic ladder. Such lecturers include many people from the local community—businessmen, town planners, conservationists— who not only lecture, but also sit in with the permanent faculty in planning courses. Some of the teaching also is done by short-term visitors, who come for a single lecture or for several weeks or months to work on a particular ecological problem.

But the most ingenious defiance of The System is the way Green Bay is organized. It has no departments of the conventional kind, controlling budgets, hiring, promotions, and courses of study. Instead the university is organized into four "theme colleges" and one school of professional studies, each granting its own kind of degree. A student, moreover, does not "major" in a traditional subject, such as chemistry or economics. Instead he concentrates on an environmental problem of his own choice, and (in consultation with his faculty advisers) selects whatever courses may help him in mastering it.

For example, if a youngster is seeking a degree in the College of Community Sciences, he might decide to concentrate on regional planning. The problem that interests him is: "How should the Lake Michigan District—nine counties in the northeastern part of Wisconsin— plan its future development?" To come up with answers, he will have to learn a good deal about economics, geography, political science, and sociology; and at some point he may find he needs some training in statistics and the use of computers. Much of his work will be done in the field, with residents and public officials of those nine counties.

If, instead, he is interested in problems of water pollution—a matter of deep concern in that region—he would enroll in the College of Environmental Sciences; and in trying to solve the particular problem he is concentrating on, he probably would dig into chemistry, hydrology, geology, and some aspects of engineering.

More than any university I have seen elsewhere, Green Bay is integrated into the surrounding community. Traditionally, research, teaching, and "extension work" or "community outreach" are regarded as separate—and sometimes hostile—enterprises. At Green Bay they all meld together.

How this works can be observed at Lake Noquebay, the main asset of Marinette County. It attracts much of the tourist trade, the county's chief source of income; and the lake is sick. It is showing symptoms of eutrophication, or premature aging. Water weeds are growing so fast that they discourage fishermen, who are getting fed up with snagged lines and clogged propellers. Besides, swimmers occasionally break out in an itchy rash which may (or may not) be caused by a tiny parasite which burrows into their skin.

This presented an ideal problem for the university's environmentalists. They are now trying to find out what causes the lake's troubles, and how to cure them. The undertaking combines scholarly research, teaching, and cooperation with the people of Marinette County to rescue their economy, all at the same time. It also demands a multidisciplinary effort—the joint work of scholars in several fields—which is one of the distinguishing characteristics of the Green Bay experiment. Thus the Noquebay project is directed by T. W. Thompson, an aquatic biologist. His faculty helpers include an analytic chemist, an economist, a water-recreation specialist, a terrestrial biologist, a political scientist, and a marine geologist. Eleven students are now working with them, and others probably will join the group from time to time. Within a year or two they hope to have two end-products: (1) a plan for the future management of the lake and its surrounding land; and (2) data which may serve as a model for similar work on other ailing lakes in the North Central states and Canada.

Such multidisciplinary undertakings often get lip service at the traditional universities, but they seldom come to much. For under the established system, a faculty member earns no academic Brownie points for this kind of enterprise. His department will regard it as time stolen from research in his own narrow specialty; and as soon as he realizes that his career may be endangered, the prudent scholar will drift away from the multidisciplinary project, however urgent and innovative it may be. The Green Bay professors may also suffer. An economist who spends a couple of years poking around a lake, instead of writing abstruse little papers for the professional journals, may not get so many job offers from other institutions. But so far the Green Bay faculty seems willing to accept this risk, as a small price to pay for the chance to take part in an exciting experiment.

Indeed, Weidner makes it plain that the teachers on his campus will have to sacrifice a lot of academic sacred cows and customs. At a breakfast meeting with the faculty just before the new university opened its doors, he told them:

> We must give up the comfortable old idea that professors meet their classes and post office hours (two or three hours a week) and then hide the rest of the week. . . . Of course you must have formal office hours. But we are at the time now when we should be available the clock around. If a month goes past and you have not had any students in your home, then there is something wrong with your approach to students. And if a week goes past and you have not had coffee with some students, if you have not got lost in some of our new people pockets with some students, then there is something wrong. . . . If any of us are uncomfortable with students outside the classroom, then we ought to find another job, because the time is gone when higher education is a thing that takes place in the classroom.

This, I take it, is precisely what thousands of students across the country have been trying to say for the last ten years, only to find that practically nobody was listening.

People pockets?

Yes, they are a unique feature of the architecture of the university buildings now going up along the shore of the bay—an architecture as remarkable as the academic plan. Because the Wisconsin winters are pretty severe, the three main buildings are linked together with passageways. But these are nothing like the straight eight-foot corridors which make hospitals and office buildings so dreary. They follow the terrain, at some points running underground, at others with windows opening on sunken gardens. And every few yards one side or the other of the passageway broadens into a little alcove, with a low table and a few easy chairs—a "people pocket" where students and faculty can stop to talk, sip a Coke, study, or just rest. The name is a little too cute for my taste, but as a device for encouraging easy, informal interaction among students and their teachers, these pockets are proving highly successful. Nice places for courting, too.

The architecture and site planning of the campus deserves an article of its own, and I hope Ada Louise Huxtable will write it one of these days. . . .

Electronic teaching is being developed at Green Bay more boldly than at any other place I know of. Its four campuses, scores of miles apart, made this almost a necessity. Last November, professors on the main Green Bay campus began lecturing not only to their own classes, but to students on the Marinette campus fifty miles to the north, using a closed-circuit television hookup provided by a grant from a local firm, the Ansul Company. Later, it may be extended to the Fox Valley campus to the west and the Manitowoc campus to the south. Meanwhile, the latter two get video tape recordings, and their students can take part in group discussions of each lecture with students on other campuses by means of a conference-line telephone network. The resulting economies are impressive. In the pilot project, a freshman course in social environment, six instructors taught some eight hundred students. Their lectures were recorded for use in future years—or for review by any student who thinks he missed something the first time.

In addition, the university has a Media Library which vastly extends the possibilities for independent study. There a student can check out a portable television set and take it to a study carrel, along with video tapes on a wide range of subjects. He also can borrow language records, audio tapes, filmstrips, and cassettes, for use at his convenience; and if he is slow to grasp something he can replay that segment as often as he likes. Some of this material is produced in the library's own television and recording studios, but much of it comes from other sources. For example, a single page of its catalogue lists ten Encyclopaedia Britannica films on the human body—"The Heart in Action," "The Perception of Sound"—plus items on caste in an Indian village, mollusks, tundra ecology, Samuel Beckett, and the behavior patterns of a one-year-old child. In length they range from an eight-minute film loop to an hour-plus "documentary report on one woman's step-by-step recovery from mental illness."

With faculty guidance, a student could get a pretty thorough (though lonesome) education in the Media Library alone, working at his own pace and without ever stepping into a classroom. One of the librarians pointed out another advantage.

"Machines," he remarked, "don't have tenure. We can replace anything here as soon as it gets obsolescent."

This may give the impression that learning at Green Bay is mechanical and dehumanized. In fact, it is so personal and student-oriented that, in comparison, the old-fashioned universities seem to be operated for the convenience of the faculty. From the day he arrives, a student finds all the individual counseling he wants, on his studies, personal problems, and future career. Remedial work, usually on a tutorial basis, is available if he needs it. If he is bothered by the usual grading system, he can, in most courses, ask to be marked simply "pass" or "fail." When he feels that he already is well-prepared in a given subject, he can ask for an examination and, if he passes, get full credit even though he has never set foot in the classroom. Required courses are few, and honors students automatically are exempted from them.

Normally, however, every student takes part in a Liberal Education Seminar during each of his four years at Green Bay. These seminars, of twelve to fifteen students each, are intended to link their specialized studies with the broader problems of society, its value systems, and the environment. They are conducted largely by the undergraduates themselves, though one or two faculty members usually are standing by to answer questions or, when necessary, to nudge the discussion back on the track.

In the sophomore year, students are encouraged to take on off-campus projects—part-time work in a local paper mill, perhaps, or a job in a reformatory, a day-care center, or a poverty program.

Juniors are expected to get some experience in a culture different from that of the Northern Great Lakes region. Depending on their interests, they might spend a few months on a campus in another part of the country, on an Indian reservation, or traveling with a small group of students and faculty members in Europe or Latin America. The purpose, in both years, is to make sure that their academic work is intimately related to the outside world. As one professor put it, "By the time he leaves here, we hope a graduate will not only understand the ecological crises the world is facing. We hope he also will have decided what he can do to help solve them."

Education: The Crisis of an Environment

BARRY N. SCHWARTZ

In preparing this volume, I spent long hours searching through the seemingly endless writings on educational philosophy, psychology, and methodology, hoping to glean that rare essay that would shed light on our topic. But nowhere among the material did I find the requisite concern for the actual environment in which education is supposed to take place. Although much attention is paid to matters of curricula, classroom procedures, the role of the teacher, and the priorities in teaching, there is only passing reference to the environmental questions that have bothered me for some time as I have tried to improve my own teaching abilities.

Just about every journal and book begins by discussing what should or should not happen after the teacher enters the room. Almost everywhere it is assumed that education is what happens between teacher and student, exclusive of other factors. But it seems to me that the educational environment itself is an important variable within the educational process. For this reason I began to consider what happens *before* the teacher enters the room.

I asked one of my classes to imagine that a Martian had landed in our classroom. Unfortunately, after only three minutes a leak developed in his spacesuit and he was forced to return to the mother ship. He had made only a cursory examination of the American school—an examination that took place before either the students or the teacher had entered the room. Still, he was required to make a report on the educational system to his superiors. I asked my class to imagine what his report would say, if anything, based as it was on the little data he had collected. My class, not unaccustomed to my Martian ploys, was willing to see through the Martian's eyes, to try to understand education solely from observation of the educational environment itself.

Typically, our discussion was reserved at first. But later it welled with enthusiasm. One student pointed out the presence of the blackboard. What did the blackboard mean? We concluded that it was there to receive information. The desk in the front of the room and the rows of chairs told us that there were two kinds of human beings in the room: one who sat up front and others who sat on the many chairs lined up through the rest of the room. The human at the front was probably special, set apart from the others, a "somebody" (a teacher). It was visually apparent that the blackboard was the receptacle of the "somebody's" information. The rest of the humans sat in chairs that were different from the "somebody's." From their design it was evident that they could be used as a place to write down the information that was placed on the blackboard. This observation was reinforced by the fact that all the chairs faced the blackboard and the "somebody," while the "somebody's" desk faced all the other people.

At this point we felt we could safely assume that what happened occurred exclusively between teacher and students, since communication among those sitting in the chairs was nearly impossible. The designer's assumption must have been that students have nothing to learn from each other or they would never have been seated so that each face spoke to the back of another student's head.

Another fact to emerge was that the teacher had much greater freedom—to move, to release energy, to be free—while the others found it awkward to leave their chairs. Since the chairs were placed close to each other, the only plausible position was a seated one. The students were fixed in their chairs, the teacher was free to walk and pace about. The teacher's mobility and the students' inactivity were built into the design of the room.

Of course, the reader might object, "When I go to the classroom, I immediately ask my students to move the chairs into a circle." What this reader forgets is that however effective a deviation from the design might be, the design itself presupposes certain *values*. These values constitute a communication to both student and teacher and they are central to what happens in the classroom.

My students (*my* students!) were not content with these observations. By this time they were seizing on every physical aspect of the environment. The walls were drab and totally without decoration. "But what," I asked, "is decoration?" They replied that it was what people did when they wished to enhance a space aesthetically, that decoration made a person feel warm and comfortable. The students concluded that it was not generally thought desirable to have students feel at home, warm, and comfortable in their educational environment. More observations of this nature followed. The ultimate conclusion was that many facets of the physical surroundings contributed to the depersonalization of the environment. The students felt that every way students might signify their relationship to each other, to their education, and to their teacher was ruled out by the physical environment itself.

Others noticed that the coat rack, the flooring, and the materials of the walls all suggested transience. Another noticed that the lighting was efficient, but that no one would have such lights in his home, except perhaps in a basement workroom. "And why not?" I asked. "Because," they answered, "the lights lack warmth; they are hard and cold."

Other aspects of the environment were seen to be durable and efficient, but with no "human" qualities. Finally, one student said that what bothered him about these physical features was that the room lacked identity. It was as if the students were simply placed there and had no way of personalizing their presence. I asked if they thought it was important to signify their presence in an environment and they unanimously agreed that it was vital. They could think of no other place where young people congregated that was devoid of youthful alteration of the environment. My own observation at this point was that the design of the room and the values that had produced it were *alien* to the needs, aspirations, and life styles of students. Another student remarked with insight that the room was antithetical to what I had once said education was all about. "If education was supposed to change a person or a group of persons and if thinking and doing were not exclusive of each other, how could that happen," he asked, "in an environment that allowed no change at all?" "Like what?" I asked. "Like changing around the room," he answered, "or the decorations or something."

In time there was no space that had not been analyzed. My class and I had engaged in a process I call the study of situational values. Each environment, by the way it is designed, tells us certain things about the designer's assumptions and values. What is so surprising here is that the assumptions underlying classroom design are antithetical to what many teachers say education should be. The primary assumption is that students are passive—in the way they learn and in the space they occupy. Ironically, I have rarely seen a teacher or any learner get excited about an idea without displaying rapid movements and a certain amount of agitated body motion. How many teachers, when they reach the focal point of their lectures, free themselves from their desks to walk, pace, and swing their bodies around? Students, however, even though they may be more generally energetic, are expected to learn while continuously immobile. The seat is a discipline over which neither the teacher nor the student has control. Though insight is the brother of energy and often the product of comfort, the physical environment remains oppressive for the students.

Another assumption that is revealed by the design of the educational environment is the belief that interaction between learners and the environment is not an important part of education. Decoration, class activity, spontaneous games, group dynamics, team efforts, and group theater do not seem to be considered germane to learning. If they were, we would have a very different kind of classroom. Even if students *are* given an opportunity for physical expression—doing—it is usually under the auspices of such fragmented educational releases as physical education—volleyball, fencing, running around a field—or art classes where, they are informed, they are supposed to make art or, worse, to learn about it. The students know, however, that they are in a static space and consequently they regard teachers as egocentric beings who behave as the only dynamos in the educational process.

It does strike me as odd that we think of the interaction of bodies in sex as an intimate experience, while the interaction of minds is thought not to need warmth or personalized location. But the facts are clear: Before the teacher even enters the room the students are situationally impressed with the divorce between thought and action, between learning and doing, between passivity and the freedom outside of school.

It is sad to think of the teacher who informs his students that the course will be a product of their collaboration and that they are free to influence the direction of learning, yet who remains unaware of the hidden values that subvert his professed egalitarian ideals.

The ability to personalize the environment may have much more to do with learning than one suspects. In any case, a first tenet of affirmative education is that such preexisting values as the environmental ones be minimized. If students wish to personalize the environment, transform it, brighten it, or give it some group identity, that must be their prerogative. After all, isn't the place for them?

Of course, there are larger implications here as well. Instead of necessitating the study of human activities as artificial and ineffective segments, a different kind of environment could make it possible to provide diversity in learning experiences while at the same time bringing unity to the student's life style. The environment could become a living and ever-changing record of the students' and teacher's fluctuating perceptions. Part of what is required is the long-heralded but largely unrealized "revolution" in the use of audio-visual materials. The use of video equipment in the classroom, for example, can alter the entire environment. Better than a roomful of mirrors, video allows the students and the teacher to experience themselves experiencing. It changes minds. Yet the use of video has thus far been minimal.

There are innumerable ways in which students could alter the school environment to promote learning. Have you ever tried to teach a course in eighteenth-century poetry by having students look at eighteenth-century paintings, listen to baroque music, even don the clothing of the period or paint rococo ornaments in watercolor on their chairs? I haven't. Under existing conditions it would simply be too difficult. The environment offers so little possibility for students to explore the experiences they are allowed to read about.

Since one of the principles of affirmative education is that students should be encouraged to correlate cognitive learning with experiential activities, the environmental situation is extremely depressing. The present absurdity is that the teacher who makes full use of the room is cited for improper conduct in the classroom. The teacher who respects the boundaries of physical space and traditional classroom procedure tends to require memorization of facts.

The whole is greater than the sum of its parts. An integrated approach to learning would be of greater benefit to students than the unending cumulative fragmentation of modern practice. But for integrated learning to succeed, the environment as it now stands must be eliminated. It is too potent an obstacle to the unsure curiosity of the young mind.

Other aspects of the physical space also call for scrutiny. Use of space and the design of the room are directly related to class size, class hours, the schedule for learning, and the idea that learning takes place in segments of time between tests. Fortress-like school structures lead to a self-fulfilling prophecy as they later come under siege.

Affirmative education requires an environment as flexible as the learners themselves, an environment that serves the interests of the students as well as those of the efficiency experts. Schools take up the single most important block of time in a young person's life. It is time schools began to resemble the places in which young people live.

§ EPILOGUE

The selections in this book lean toward educational reform. Most of the writers are acquainted with existing school systems and advocate redirecting the present system to obtain more satisfying results. These are men who, if you will, seek realistic ways of making life more valuable to young people during the years of their education. Another point of view holds that educational reform is a poor compromise with an unworkable system. Proponents of this view argue that there cannot be meaningful education within an institutional framework. Since this more radical position offers few if any workable options to the present educational system, it is seldom given a great deal of attention.

At present affirmative education is an idea, a hope, and, occasionally, a reality. A complete reevaluation of contemporary education and its implications has yet to be carried out. In this epilogue we can begin that exploration.

The two pieces that follow involve radical questioning of our assumptions. Affirmative education is seen as a transition between existing structures and an eventual complete transformation of the whole idea of education. Both Illich and Disch look forward to a time when the institutions to which we now entrust the education of our young will no longer exist.

Few people are better qualified to engage in such radical questioning than Ivan Illich. Illich has distinguished himself in numerous articles and in his recent book, *DeSchooling Society*, as a pioneer in formulating educational requirements of the future. For Illich, no real change can occur until individuals are freed from the institutions that now control their lives. Although it may be said that Illich's suggestions are too remote to be taken seriously, many find themselves in enthusiastic agreement with his argument that there can be no learning until it is separated from schools and integrated with life experience. His concept of deschooling and decentralization of educational resources harks back to a time when one learned by experiential means and by self-motivated energies.

Perhaps the straw that may someday break the institutional back of the educational system will be the demise of faith in literacy as the only path to learning. Certainly in the past decade strong voices have been raised—among them Buckminster Fuller and Marshall McLuhan —to argue that the generation maturing in the technological era is discovering new sensory modes of experience and new media through which perceptions are developed and cognitive learning is achieved.

Robert Disch, whose background is literary, leads us into a probing encounter with the present reliance on literacy as the major tool for learning. If McLuhan's point—that some societies will altogether skip the literacy stage as they move from preliterate to electronic media stages—is correct, then current concepts of education will be short-lived.

These two essays are offered as an epilogue because they offer a vision of the future of educational developments. Though they cannot be documented, considering their points can do much to help us understand the requirements of the future—an understanding that is necessary if education is, indeed, to be affirmative.

Deschooling:

A CONVERSATION WITH IVAN ILLICH

Barry Schwartz: Perhaps it would be helpful at the outset if **you** would define and elaborate your concept of deschooling.

Ivan Illich: You know, it is a ghastly thing, this coining of new words. I almost wish I had not spoken of deschooling. Do you know where I learned it? There was a meeting in the Urban Training Center in Chicago. It's a very good place. There was a group of people from the Black Economic Development Corporation and I was supposed to discuss something with them. Well, I started to tease some of them because of the consumer orientation in their development plans. And when we spoke of school I wanted to try to get from them what people really feel schools do. Finally the real words came up. And at a certain moment some guy said, "Yeah, you are right. Schools are made to screw you." But I understood that he had said schools are made to school you. When I repeated this everybody laughed, because this was evidently not what the guy had said. In the afternoon we all showed up with buttons: "School you." We then began to speak of the deschooling of society.

But look here, I have just come from Peru. One half-hour after landing in Peru, I faced for three or four hours a group of 500 teachers. These teachers were in the fourth month of retraining as trainers of other teachers from all over Peru in the deschooling of Peruvian society. A crazy situation! Under a military government! I met a colonel who is Secretary of Education and Colonel of Public Relations who gave me instructions on how to walk up to the microphone: Seventeen steps from here and you will stand two steps to the left and one step back, where the microphone will be hung over your neck. Yet, even with that kind of men in charge, I find a group of 500 teachers who during the four months of study use as their main texts for reading some of the articles and basic papers from Cidoc, some Marcuse, and some John Holt—the later writings. A group of 500 people who have come to the conclusion that professional teaching is of questionable legitimacy as a profession, that obligatory schooling has to be abolished as soon as possible if some kind of equality of access to educational opportunities is to become possible, that a major battle must be started against licensing in the fields of health, education, welfare, accounting, and law.

So to my greatest surprise, in Peru, under a military government, I found the first major nationwide movement toward the deschooling of society.

Schwartz: By deschooling, you mean here the decentralization of educational structures?

Illich: Yes, and the elimination of any discrimination when you apply for a job on the basis of previous consumption of school years.

Schwartz: So it is no longer a criterion for the evaluation of the worth of a person?

Illich: Yes, and it means serious questioning of the necessity of any kind of previous schooling for a person who wants to teach. It means the abolition, therefore, of any pretense at obligatory school attendance in a country in which the entire national budget would not be sufficient to provide for each person three years in school. It means a very serious threat to further expenditures on university students. It is an absurd situation that the more you climb the school pyramid the more money per year should be spent on you. One would think that less and less would be necessary as people become more and more capable of learning by themselves.

I am not aware of any country in the world where you have 500 teachers gathered in the Ministry of Education asking these radical questions—not in Russia or in the United States or in Cuba or Chile.

Schwartz: What about application of this idea in the United States? In the United States we have the extraordinary situation of, on the one hand, a pervasive feeling that schools are meaningless, that schools are used to forestall a generation from entering the labor market, while on the other hand, there is less meaningful work available and less labor needed. What do you do in a situation where, if you deschool free individuals, the society is incapable of absorbing them?

Illich: Well, if you really wish to raise that question one must go into a further analysis of what a commodity is. I think there Marx is quite correct in the first chapters of *Das Kapital*. He said that through the concept of commodity you get the best insight into the structure of society. But in Marx's time a commodity was mostly a thing that was made. In our society it is not the thing made but the intangible service rendered that constitutes the overwhelming commodity in which the production and consumption of our society is involved. Marx saw this, but the Marxists didn't understand it.

The nontangible commodity, called a service, can be quantified, purchased, accumulated—just think of the way school years are accumulated—and constitutes the fulcrum of contemporary nontangible capitalism in which East and West share equally. I do believe that the real consumer today is not so much the man who needs to smoke or eat or have a new car; rather, what makes him a consumer is that he believes neither he nor anyone else will be human unless he consumes a lot of service. I think it is only recently, about 400 or 500 years ago, that we found out people were born dumb and needed education to be able to enter bourgeois society. I think that we will not come to a radical criticism of the consumer society until we have unmasked the commodity characteristics of health, education, and welfare in society today.

Schwartz: Are you including the role of the intellectual, per se?

Illich: Yes, he produces a knowledge commodity. An otherwise brilliant man, Kenneth Boulding, speaks of the growth of the knowledge stock, happening so fast that very soon the transmission of the stock from one generation to the other will take more effort and will consume more energy than men will have available for further adding to that knowledge stock. We believe that somehow the intellectual is a stockholder in the international knowledge stock.

Now, the issue that you raised about the artificial creation of unemployment, or the nontangible pollution of the world through the production and consumption of nontangible commodities, cannot be faced unless we do an exact analysis, if you want just to give it a name, following Marx, but applying it almost exclusively to the nontangible commodity of our economy, because unemployment is the *sad* inactivity of a man. Not all inactivity is sad. But this is the sad inactivity of a man who has unlearned to enjoy leisure, creativity, interpersonal relationship and for whom there is nothing to make, neither tangible goods nor intangible values. Inevitably, in a society that is populated by people who have unlearned to enjoy leisure, have unlearned really to enjoy each other, and where machines can produce increasingly more tangible commodities with increasingly less investment of manpower, we have to invent some kinds of ever new intangible commodities, such as education, and define everybody as either a producer or a consumer of education. So when I speak about the deschooling of society, the deschooling of the mind, what I suggest is a freeing of the individual from believing in the value of institutionally produced or consumed education, health, welfare, whatever it might be.

Schwartz: Marcuse talks about the technological rationality that is a function most often fulfilled by intellectuals, professionals, and so on. The mystification of experience, and of course deschooling, is, in one sense, a consciousness or an attitude that frees oneself from those who translate experiences for us.

Illich: Yes. You know there is an insight that I wish people would try to begin to feel in the words used in this conversation: I don't know enough about psychology to dare speak about this with authority. But I do believe that there is a strange institutionalization of an oedipal relationship in modern symbiotic man in his attitude toward alma mater. All over the United States students are gathering to devise new curricula by which they would be "schooled" and ultimately trying to become themselves teachers, making it, making alma mater in one form or another. Perhaps it is called a free school. To be educated, bring forth, educate, generate their own children; the *oedipus dedascolos*—oedipus the teacher—is perhaps rooted much deeper than anyone until now has been willing to point out in a society that has institutionalized values. Even where the students don't even want a degree they still want education.

Now, one of the things I am working on presently is a little bit of historical research. I have discovered, much to my surprise, that the word *education* had originally a purely alchemic meaning—up until the fifteenth century. It meant educe, bring forth; in this case, gold from the original slime. *Education* was used only as a word by hermetic alchemists who wanted to compel the base elements of this world —just look at our slums—to compel them up level by level through graduations (another alchemic word), up toward enlightenment, to make them into gold by adding on each level the appropriate matter, the precipitate as they called it, sulphur, to the basic mercury. In fact, they spoke about torturing the base elements to make them into gold. *Education* was used only in this connection—to educe or educate—in all European languages, including Latin, in the fourteenth and thirteenth centuries. The old Latin word, *educatios prolis*, which did exist, meant nurturing a baby.

Education appears for the first time in French, a modern language, in 1497, the same year Erasmus settled in Oxford. *Education* had nothing to do with learning. The word *education* appears in English in 1530 or so (that is what the *Oxford Dictionary* says) but in Spanish eighty years after the University of Lima was founded, some sixty or seventy years after the University of Mexico was founded. Lope de

Vega speaks about the word *education* as a neologism and the concept as some crazy innovation. But history seems to indicate that the idea that all people are born dumb and cannot fit into human society until they have received a certain amount of education is nothing but a secularization of the pre-Reformation idea that all people are born sinners and must be baptized before they can be accepted into civilized European society. And in fact, only after the Reformatory Wars of the sixteenth century and seventeenth century did all people, Christian and non-Christian alike, believe that all people are born dumb, a new form of original sin, and must receive some ritual treatment before they can become citizens. So if you are saying to me that most people who are engaged in educational reform at this moment still aim at some kind of certification, I would say you might be right, but there are already groups around that say to hell with certificates—the hell with education.

The way I try to deal with addicted people here at the Center is that here you have the possibility of listing in the catalog the name of the person and the thing he wants to treat—no questions asked. As long as he states clearly what he wants to talk about, we know people will come to his class believing that they can now play at some kind of free school, so we impose three rules: a teacher should let himself be examined by his prospective students for two hours so that nobody sticks with him for the rest of class who hasn't found him interesting; we exclude operational organization of the subversion of Mexican institutions so as to be able to say to police that it is not our fault if somebody does it during class hours; and the third rule is that there be no classroom behavior that the majority of the gardeners would consider lewd.

Now, we try to make the place as agreeable as possible so that people can sit down in corners and do what anyway is the only valuable thing around most universities—the informal meetings around a cup of coffee. The more I think about it the less I believe in education. A year ago I still would have said that I am speaking in favor of education and therefore condemning schools. But now I have realized that the very idea of education is a myth to which the ritual of schooling corresponds. But I must have the courage to say we don't want education because education is always something alienating. We want a meaningful world, a world where everyone can learn from living.

Schwartz: And not the environments that distort people?

Illich: Well, what does distort people? Environments in which we do not radically limit some dimensions of progress. Let me stay with one of the most simple ones, say speed. And I will speak of Latin America. I do know that if in Latin America we radically limit speeds to ten miles per hour, less than 0.5 percent of the people who travel for more than five hours would move slower than they now move. There are not more than one out of two hundred people who more than five times in a year move over the distance of ten miles in less than an hour. So practically nobody's interest would be hurt. So if we have a ten miles per hour speed limit nobody in the world would have an interest of possessing a tool, a vehicle, that moves faster than ten miles per hour. It would be stupid; and a vehicle that moves at ten miles per hour can not cost more than $150, a maximum of $200 per item. And the roadbed upon which a beast such as a mechanical donkey moves costs only one percent of that which a hard surface, all-weather road built for speeds of seventy miles and weights of five thousand kilos costs. But if at the same time you had ten-mile-per-hour cars, people would get used to them very fast. And in no time you would have nobody in that town who would not be able to repair such motors. And the most modern technology that can be incorporated in such motors would give them five times the life expectancy of a Model T.

Schwartz: But isn't it often argued by Latin Americans that the problem is not that they are moving too fast, but rather that the rate of change is so terribly slow?

Illich: Look, at this moment we need people who have the guts to answer this question: "It's easy for you to speak about deschooling society, or about cutting out the medical profession, layizing medicine completely, making modern knowledge available to everybody, but after all you wouldn't be where you are without your university studies and perhaps you wouldn't have survived."

Schwartz: That's not my question, but if you like you can answer it.

Illich: It takes a much nastier form in the *ad hominem* argument. But my answer would be that we are by no means moving too slowly in technological development, but we are moving much too fast for much too few. You see the class structure of society today is not determined by the possession of money per se, or goods, but by the previous consumption of intangible services. All over the world we justify the idea that the technocrat has the right to greater speeds, more medical support, more secretarial services, because he is so valuable.

Schwartz: Well, the whole notion of the worth of an individual is based on the degree to which the machine is served.

Illich: Exactly; it is only through the radical attack on the idea that progress somehow entitles one to more expensive tools or that more expensive tools can serve more people, but only if they are handled by appropriate technocrats. And this idea is very disturbing for most people.

Schwartz: I wonder if you would elaborate on the practice of what sounds so correct as a theory.

Illich: Of course I don't have any answers on a world-wide basis. But there are some implications of which we don't have to be afraid. We must question the common sense, humanity, and morality of people who bring children into this world in, say, New York City. (I know this sounds terrible, but I thought about this very clearly; I was shocked only for a minute), but I was just in South America for three days; at one point an American—very enlightened, the best kind of left-wing liberal, still in an important position in this department —asked to see me, and he made a remark about how cruel it was to bring children into this world in Lima Barriotas. Well, there is no comparison to the inhumanity, the gilded inhumanity in which middle-class children have to grow up in New York; that metallic plastic environment in which we rarely see anything that hasn't been planned, hasn't been put there by design. As Monsiegnor Bob Fox once said to me: "You are wrong; there are some things that aren't planned there —for example, puddles and banana peels." There is no comparison between the inhumanity of putting the human being in the circumstance of having to grow up in New York and of having to grow up in Lima.

These are the questions we have to ask. May we carefully breed one generation after another of whites and, in the U.S., equal numbers of black men, who perpetuate new generations without resistance, without ability to live in a normal human environment? That is a probable generation of sick people. May we inflict on the rest of the world poisoning of the atmosphere, of the radiation levels of the sea, in order then to be able to preserve these dehumanized man-made human beings? These are issues that have to be raised. A kid who has been born into New York, who has to survive that—all we can say is that even in the concentration camps one could live humanly. One can survive humanly. Those of us who have had that experience know.

Schwartz: Tough question.

Beyond Literacy

ROBERT DISCH

Before the last decade the assumption that literacy should be the central or core factor in education was seldom questioned. Although other topics were included in the curriculum and "audio-visuals" were used to supplement textbooks, educators nevertheless understood their primary objective to be the teaching of reading and writing and the subsequent application of these literary skills to other academic subjects. In the 1950s and '60s both parents and educators became very disturbed about *Why Johnny Can't Read* while remaining relatively unconcerned with his ability to think, feel, or fix his car. In fact, the primacy of literacy in education was as firmly established as medieval cosmology before Copernicus or Newtonian physics before quantum theory.

In recent years a number of important developments have begun to challenge the idea of literacy as the keystone of the educational structure. In my opinion these developments will effect important changes in our assumptions regarding the relationship between education and literacy.

Among the many interrelated factors that will affect the future of literacy are: (1) The growing and irreversible impact of audio-visual methods of communication. The widespread use of the telephone, for example, has diminished the ability to write sentences. Worldwide satellite systems could be used to raise world literacy levels, but it is more likely that the antiliteracy bias of such audio-visual communication methods will decrease the need for literacy by dispensing information through audio-visual media and thereby further lower the prestige and quality of writing. (2) Greater interest in sensory and awareness training, touch/feel therapies, and other forms of physical communication that make little use of literacy. (3) The rejection of traditional values and goals by many young people and the effort to establish alternative life styles—as with the street people, communal farmers, craftsmen, and so forth—that place little value on literary skill. (4) The influence of Marshall McLuhan, Buckminster Fuller, Norman O. Brown, and other prophets of technology, cybernation, design solutions, and radical Freudianism, all of whom in one way or another turn against the culture that is, rightly or wrongly, assumed to be dependent upon and structured by literacy. (5) The emphasis in modern linguistics on the primacy of oral over written language.

For the sake of argument let us suppose that these factors taken together suggest that Western society is moving toward a non- or quasi-literate state, toward a stage of development in which the conditions necessary to sustain a sophisticated form of written communication have disappeared.

These assumptions would certainly be supported by English teachers, who for years have not only failed to teach students to write effective prose, but have themselves shown diminished powers of composition (if one is to judge by the quality of formal prose that appears in scholarly journals).[1]

This would not be the first time in history that sophisticated human skills were lost. Nor would it be the first fierce and perhaps hopeless struggle to prevent the inevitable from occurring. The failure of Renaissance humanists to bring Ciceronian Latin into popular use and the futility of the various attempts to imitate classical architecture reveal how difficult it is to control cultural movements. Often the very struggle to impose cultural norms results in the loss of valuable cultural property. According to Norbert Wiener, the Renaissance effort to substitute Ciceronian elegance for the simpler and widely used medieval vernacular resulted only in the death of medieval Latin. "For this sin of pride," he explains, "we now have to pay in the absence of an adequate international language far superior to the artificial ones such as Esperanto, and well suited for the demands of the present day." [2]

Despite the warnings from the past, research seldom investigates the future of literacy. Charles Silberman has written that "students now starting school may still be in the labor force in the year 2030; they need an education that will prepare them, or enable them to be prepared, for jobs whose very nature cannot now even be imagined." Yet most educators have neglected to think about programs that would consider the needs of a postliterate society.

There are many important reasons why a critique of literacy has been so long in arriving. Literacy is wrapped in such a protective

1. Readers who doubt that university-level composition courses fail to teach composition should review the many articles on the subject that have appeared during the past few years in *College English.*

2. Norbert Wiener, *Cybernetics and Society: The Human Use of Human Beings* (New York: Doubleday, Anchor Books, 1954), pp. 88–91.

mantle of respectability, sanctity, and presumed goodness that it has developed a powerful mystique of its own. When open-minded inquiry focuses on the question of literacy *qua* literacy panic and confusion often follow.

There are, of course, real historical and cultural factors behind these reactions. For the sake of simplicity I will review some of these influences separately, but most are interrelated.

As is well known, the rise of the middle class in England in the late seventeenth and throughout the eighteenth centuries, and the ultimate ascendancy of this class to political and economic power, was linked with slowly rising literacy rates. Literacy became a distinguishing characteristic of the bourgeoisie; it separated the middle-class individual from his lower-class origins and provided him with the tools he needed to conduct commerce, build his fortune, and exercise power. It is not surprising that the great middle-class novels of Defoe and Richardson—as well as the formal grammar book—made their appearance when this class was searching for ways to establish its values, confirm its identity, and define its role in the world.

Literacy, along with proper grammar and speech, quickly became the American route to social mobility, a way to demonstrate one's cultural superiority and establish a secure place in the class hierarchy. The idea of literacy as a means of "acculturation" still exerts a strong influence on the mystique of literacy. Even at this late date course descriptions and college textbooks point out that the "educated man" knows how to spell and use "correct" grammar. Earlier, the Puritans had assigned to literacy an important part in the drama of salvation. Their schools emphasized teaching children to read so they could discover for themselves the moral instruction of the Bible.

At the present time, with bourgeois values and religious institutions both undergoing major transformations, it is not strange that middle class educators would hesitate to deal with the problems raised by the changing status of literacy. But there are other, less obvious reasons for our failure to develop a rigorous critique of literacy. One is simply that the models of society constructed by liberal reformers, economists, and sociologists all place literacy and education at the center of human progress. They believe that a combination of increased social mobility and higher levels of education would make American institutions work more effectively, solve the major social problems, and generate a situation in which social conflict would be minimal and ideology superfluous. Hence it is obvious that progressive and liberal thinkers cannot be expected to develop a critique of literacy that might conflict with their interpretation of the functioning and overall progress of liberal democratic society.

On a scale far more widespread than liberal theory is the complex set of attitudes about Western cultural and racial superiority that feed into the mystique of literacy. Many people believe that it is literacy—rather than speech—that separates man from the "beast," and that civilization depends on literacy for its continued existence. To lose literacy would thus be to sink to the "animal level." Likewise, feelings of cultural superiority in the West are tied to both technological superiority and literary sophistication. These ideas in turn fuel the machine that allows the highly developed nations to wreak havoc on the peoples and cultures of other lands. The fact that a culture or some of its people do not read, write, or possess elaborate technology seems to grant license for exploitation.

Along with the belief that the most "advanced" societies are also the literate societies comes the idea that literacy is both symptom and cause of the inevitable progress of all mankind from barbarism into the "civilized" state. This worldwide historical development is held to be desirable because it allows people to free themselves from enslavement to superstition and "savage" practices. Similar ideas about the efficacy of literacy to save the world are held by many humanists and scholars, who believe in salvation through the study of the great ideas in the great books. By mastering literacy and applying oneself to the wisdom of the past, one learns to think independently, to make sense out of the present, and to function effectively in the world. This overly familiar rhetoric is dutifully recited to freshmen in September and to seniors in June.

Some nonacademics fear the deterioration of literacy because they know what literacy has meant in their lives. As a result they feel a genuine responsibility to see that others will be able to share their experiences. Less idealistically, many people living in poverty are naturally hostile to any questioning of the mechanisms of education by which they feel they might escape from poverty or by which they hope their children will escape in the future.

These examples by no means exhaust the components of the mystique of literacy. But they are sufficient to indicate that the idea of literacy is deeply rooted in the social, cultural, economic, religious, and class structures of modern society. To question the role of literacy is therefore to reconsider the very basis on which our society was established and on which it presently operates.

When all of these factors are put in perspective, it is easy to see why the educator would make literacy the center of education and undervalue subjects that have little or no connection with literacy. All high school students, for example, must take four years of something called "English," but courses like graphic arts, music, and crafts are usually given on an elective basis. In establishing such requirements the schools and their policymakers merely reflect the historical conditions from which they emerged. To begin seriously examining the traditional assumptions about literacy, we need new and different social conditions, conditions that are now beginning to influence the future of literacy.

One element that is shaping new attitudes toward literacy is the pervasive feeling—particularly among young people—that Western society has come to the end of its development and that only through a revolutionary cultural transformation will it be reborn.

Both student radicals and the literary scholar George Steiner have observed that Nazi Germany, though steeped in the traditions of humanistic learning, was still capable of genocide, that mass murders were in fact directed by lovers of Nietzsche and Mozart. Though it would be absurd to place the blame for Buchenwald (or My Lai, for that matter) on the failure of the humanistic tradition, the case of Germany does provide ammunition for those who charge that humanistic culture is morally exhausted. Many young people believe the humanistic cultural heritage to be a dubious bulwark against the insanity that modern technology can perpetrate.

In any event, the doubts about Western society that have taken shape since World War II inevitably lead to questions about the value of literacy because it is the single characteristic distinguishing modern societies from conspicuously "primitive" ones. As the values of the Western nations come under fire, curiosity about the lives of peoples in so-called primitive cultures has been renewed.

Claude Levi-Strauss, who applies the methods of structural analysis to the understanding of primitive myths and customs, shows that the untamed ("sauvage") mind of the nonliterate primitive—though keyed to the understanding of experience through reference to plants, animals, and objects found in the environment—is as complex and logical as the literate mind of the scientific Westerner. Levi-Strauss believes that all societies have parallel mental and myth-making "structures," but that social functioning is often smoother in the primitive societies. Commenting on Levi-Strauss, Sanche de Gramont points out that "if progress were based on success in founding harmonious family and social groups, the Australian Aborigines would be judged most advanced." [3]

Besides recognizing that nonliterate societies have complex patterns of mental and social life, Levi-Strauss also finds that literacy itself—the one area where parallel "structures" do not exist—has perhaps been responsible for some of the chronic human and social dislocations that affect literate societies. Contrary to the popular belief that the ability to read leads to mental liberation, critical thought, and intel-

3. This and other quotations relating to Levi-Strauss are from "There Are No Superior Societies," by Sanche de Gramont, *New York Times Magazine*, January 28, 1968.

lectual independence is the suspicion that literacy in fact creates slaves. In the words of Levi-Strauss, literacy "seems to favor the exploitation rather than the enlightenment of mankind." He charges that writing "made it possible to assemble workmen by the thousands and set them tasks which taxed them to the limit of their strength. If my hypothesis is correct, the primary function of writing, as a means of communication, is to facilitate the enslavement of other human beings." Although Levi-Strauss absolutely denies that one culture is superior to another, the implication remains that literacy is the snake in literate man's Garden of Eden. "Without going so far as to suggest a causal relationship," writes Sanche de Gramont, "Levi-Strauss links the origin of writing in the Eastern Mediterranean between the second and third millenniums to one of the constants of Western society, the exploitation of man by man."

Writers within the humanistic tradition itself have posed questions that, while not attacking literacy directly, are relentlessly critical of the culture it supports. For Professor Louis Kampf the abuses made of the literary tradition reflect the same connection between literacy and human exploitation that is feared by Levi-Strauss. In the universities, Kampf believes, the humanistic tradition is used to brainwash armies of future corporate functionaries into believing that their bureaucratic tasks are somehow meaningfully related to the past, "that these tasks are—however mysteriously—connected to Homer, the Athenians, the Judeo-Christian tradition, and the rest of our cultural baggage. The connections may not be clear, but we feel a terrible guilt if we do not perceive them." [4] The traditional liberal arts education, based on cultural history and the great books, is manipulated "to make the acculturating mechanisms more efficient," but not to "issue in any sort of activity which makes a claim to any social relevance beyond acculturation. . . . The master task of the humanities becomes one of accommodating the students to the social dislocations of industrial society." Instead of leading to a rational critique of society, "the study of our classics seems to provide us with ideological blinders. It mystifies —to use R. D. Laing's phrase—the very basis of our experience: our way of seeing, feeling, knowing. The humanities have been the educational system's unwitting collaborator in destroying our experience —that is, our humanity. For by blinding us to social mechanisms they have made us unconscious; they have made us the victims of a myth; they have kept us from seeing things as they really are. And, to quote Laing again, 'if our experience is destroyed, our behavior will be destructive.' And so it is. It is so because our culture has taught us to disguise competitive aggression as social benevolence, oppression as

4. Louis Kampf, "The Humanities and the Inhumanities," *The Nation,* September 30, 1969.

freedom, hate as love. These marvelous transformations have been effected not only by those who control our most powerful institutions but by our educators—our experts in acculturation."

Another penetrating critique of literary culture, which comments by implication on the dangers of literacy, is Susan Sontag's recent essay, "Against Interpretation." [5] Sontag argues that the act of criticism —still dominated by Platonic and Aristotelian concepts of "mimesis" —in asking art to "justify itself" through interpretation, has supplanted the direct *experience* of art, the "incantatory, [the] magical; art [as] an instrument of ritual." Though Sontag does not make this observation, the shift in artistic meaning—from experienced ritual to theory, interpretation, and justification—historically coincides with the use of literacy for expression in religion and philosophy. Arguing that Western fascination with "interpretation" has emasculated both art and criticism, she recommends a fundamental change in the uses of criticism. "In some cultural contexts, interpretation is a liberating act. It is a means of revising, or transvaluing, of escaping the dead past. In other cultural contexts, it is reactionary, impertinent, cowardly, stifling. . . . Today is such a time."

Other writers, often following in the footsteps of Marshall McLuhan, have developed educational techniques that would essentially dispense with literacy and put a new "visual culture" in its place. Although many of these writers are tortuously evasive about the role they imagine for literacy in a visually oriented society, the changes they recommend would unavoidably have profound negative implications for the future of literacy.

An important writer in this vein is Caleb Gattegno, whose works integrate the developmental theories of Jean Piaget with the media concepts of Marshall McLuhan. In his book, *Towards A Visual Culture,* Gattegno argues that "what we usually do when we think via the medium of memorized words, which form so much of our verbal education, is to generate a static universe." To break out of this static condition, Gattegno suggests the use of television and other visual media to "develop a complete visual code that feeds information without words. . . ." By moving our educational techniques completely into the realm of sensory experience, he predicts that we will expedite the coming of the new man, the new culture.

These are only a few examples from the growing critique of literacy. A complete list would naturally include, among others, McLuhan, the linguistic theories of Noam Chomsky, Buckminster Fuller's emphasis on oral and visual experience, and Norman O. Brown's radical Freudian critique of Western history, in which the literary tradition ap-

5. Susan Sontag, "Against Interpretation," from *Against Interpretation,* 1964, Farrar, Strauss and Giroux, Inc.

pears alternately as excrement and as part of "the dead hand of the past on the present" that blocks human salvation through "the resurrection of the body" and the death of "sublimation."

This growing and potent body of criticism, with its explicit and implicit demands for radical change, suggests many issues that educators and society in general will have to confront. At this point I would like to indulge in a few modest speculations about the consequences of removing literacy from its central position in Western education. I am in no sense arguing that literacy be suppressed or abolished. I am instead fantasizing about the consequences of allowing literacy to find its own place among the various modes of communication, artistic expression, perception, and experience.

LITERACY AND CULTURAL DIVERSITY

Mankind is currently experiencing a great loss through the decimation of nonliterate cultures, with their magnificent diversity and their valuable imaginative and artistic differences. Levi-Strauss comments: "It is true that ethnology is faced with the eventual disappearance of primitive societies. . . . I wonder whether, the more voluminous contemporary societies become, the more they tend to re-create within themselves the diversity they have destroyed elsewhere." Would a change in the position that literacy now holds expedite cultural transformations and thus lead to increased cultural richness and greater diversity within our own society?

LITERACY AND ART

What kind of art would a society produce if it contained people whose lives were oriented toward the "visual code" suggested by Gattegno rather than toward the static universe he insists results from the rigidities of the verbal culture? The role and function of art in any culture is essential to its diversity and the vitality of its life. Literacy has made possible the development of such powerful art forms as the novel while simultaneously destroying the oral basis of epic poetry, one of the greatest achievements of mankind. If literacy did not hold a central position in education, art would necessarily reflect different sensibilities. Quite possibly we would rediscover uses for song and oral poetry that were lost centuries ago. The current importance of rock music and its lyrics to the young may represent a tentative start in this direction. It is possible to imagine a time, in fact, when art would again be its own justification, immediately perceived and incorporated, without "interpretation"; a condition where, as Susan Sontag writes, we might find the "innocence before all theory when art knew no need to justify itself, when one did not ask of a work of art what it said because one knew (or thought one knew) what it *did*. . . . Indeed, we have an obligation to overthrow any means of defending and justifying art which becomes particularly obtuse or onerous or insensitive to contemporary needs and practice." [6]

LITERACY AND IDEAS

Scholars and specialists continually report that it is no longer possible to keep abreast of even the narrowest of fields. Phrased in terms of Gresham's Law, valuable contributions and new ideas are driven out of circulation and derivative recapitulations of dead concepts replace them. Like the furniture in Ionesco's *The New Tenant* or the "Forgotten Works" in Richard Brautigan's novel, *In Watermelon Sugar,* literacy is suffocating its audience. There is a very real possibility that ideas and insights of genius will be lost in the clutter. The development of a sensory culture will not eliminate this possibility, but it is vitally necessary to bring to the surface those ways of seeing, thinking, feeling, and being alive that are crucial to humane survival.

LITERACY AND BRAINWASHING

Kafka spoke for many readers when he said that "a book is an ax to break the frozen seas of the mind." But as Louis Kampf implied and as Nazi Germany proved, literacy used to manipulate men is a dangerous instrument. Children are profoundly influenced by the anti-art, jingoistic, racist, fear-inducing, and conformist nature of most of their reading materials. One function of literacy is obviously to create "good citizens" and "good soldiers," obedient and easily manipulated servants of the industrial empires.

Astonishing as it may sound, most schools in America do not distinguish between the values espoused by *The Reader's Digest,* and those expressed in—to select a popular example—the Greek myths. The inevitable "book reports" are ground out on the myths one week and on the *Digest's* propaganda the next. Indeed, the *Digest* ultimately exerts more influence over the student's mind than the bowdlerized Greek texts usually taught by teachers indifferent to or ignorant of everything vital in Greek literature.

To be free to read is a radical freedom, but to have this freedom perverted by commercial exploiters, government propagandists, and cultural pacifiers diminishes the claim that literacy should dominate education. The basic conflict that has surrounded literacy, especially since the development of the printing press, has always been whether

6. *Ibid.*

literacy should be used to liberate or to control. In our culture at this time, literacy would appear to serve the latter purpose.

This is not meant to propose that we abolish literacy, even if that were possible. To do so would deprive us of a needed check against other forms of manipulation. One of the fundamental assumptions of media prophets like Gattegno and McLuhan is that the new culture destined to emerge from the sensory media revolution will inevitably work beneficial changes for humanity. But there is absolutely no way of predicting what this society will be like, or that children whose minds are far more capable of comprehending and manipulating concepts and data would necessarily become more humane as adults.

LITERACY AND HUMAN GROWTH

Many children suffer emotional damage when they are forced to learn reading. As a result, many grow into adulthood with serious mental blocks about words, useless fears and feelings of inadequacy, perhaps a grovelling but uncomprehending respect for the literary establishment. If we put less weight on literacy, we might be able to provide socially and educationally acceptable ways for those children who find only torment in written language to undertake other creative and healthful tasks.

LITERACY, SCIENCE, AND TECHNOLOGY

Very little is known about the interaction between science and literacy, so speculation in this area is necessarily restricted. We need to know how the present body of scientific knowledge was shaped by its interaction with literacy. We also need to learn whether or not literacy is crucial to the experimental and theoretical aspects of "pure" science.

Some nonliterate cultures have developed brilliant levels of technology and crafts. The impact of literacy stimulated many new and fruitful developments in technology (such as the printing press and movable type), and it is likely that a very different technology would result from changed attitudes toward literacy. Would this technology be more closely tied to the senses, more humane, and less destructive of fundamental human values than our present technology?

In and of itself, education cannot generate the conditions that will allow for the renewal of the flagging spirit of Western man. Forces beyond the control of educators will contribute to the shape of the future. The goal of a better society will never be achieved if we allow the process of education to pervert the wild imagination and intensity of feeling that characterize so many of the young. If institutionalized "education" diminishes a child's ability to envision a new world, that approach fails both the present and the future.

Obviously, few agree about the nature of adult responsibility for educating youth. I am simply urging that we refuse to allow the mystique of literacy to dictate the educational milieu in which our children imagine and create the world they will inherit.